US NAVY SHIPS
VS
JAPANESE ATTACK AIRCRAFT

1941–42

MARK STILLE

OSPREY PUBLISHING
Bloomsbury Publishing Plc
PO Box 883, Oxford, OX1 9PL, UK
1385 Broadway, 5th Floor, New York, NY 10018, USA
E-mail: info@ospreypublishing.com
www.ospreypublishing.com

OSPREY is a trademark of Osprey Publishing Ltd

First published in Great Britain in 2020

A catalog record for this book is available from the British Library.

ISBN: PB 9781472836441; eBook 9781472836458; ePDF 9781472836465;
XML 9781472836472

20 21 22 23 24 10 9 8 7 6 5 4 3 2 1

Edited by Tony Holmes
All artwork by Jim Laurier
Maps and formation diagrams by www.bounford.com
Index by Sandra Shotter
Typeset by PDQ Digital Media Solutions, Bungay, UK
Printed and bound in India by Replika Press Private Ltd

Osprey Publishing supports the Woodland Trust, the UK's leading woodland
conservation charity.

To find out more about our authors and books visit:
www.ospreypublishing.com. Here you will find extracts, author interviews,
details of forthcoming events and the option to sign up for our newsletter.

D3A1 "Vals" attacking USS *Lexington* (CV-2) cover art

On May 8, 1942, during the Battle of the Coral Sea, 33 D3A1 "Vals" were
part of a 69-strong IJNAF strike that targeted the two carriers of the US
Navy's Task Force 17. Led by *Shokaku*'s air group commander, Lt Cdr
Kakuichi Takahashi, the aircraft attacked both USS *Lexington* (CV-2) and USS
Yorktown (CV-5). The carriers were operating together, with an escort of five
heavy cruisers and seven destroyers. Despite the presence of 17 F4F Wildcats
in the general area on a combat air patrol, Takahashi's dive-bombers were able
to position themselves for an attack from an upwind position while his B5N
"Kate" torpedo-bombers descended for an immediate attack. Takahashi led the
dive-bombers himself. The first dove on their targets several minutes after the
torpedo attack, so the Japanese strike was not fully coordinated. Takahashi
detailed his 19 *Shokaku* dive-bombers to attack *Lexington* and the 14 from
Zuikaku to attack *Yorktown*. All 33 D3A1s were able to deliver their attacks,
diving from 14,000ft, unmolested by fighters. The results were very
disappointing for the Japanese, however, as although the two carriers were
deluged by splashes from bombs landing close by, only three hit the ships, and
damage was light. The only explanation for this lack of success was the heavy
antiaircraft fire put up by the Americans – *Lexington* boasted 12 5in./38 guns,
11 1.1in. quad mounts and numerous 20mm single guns.

B5N2 "Kates" attacking USS *Hornet* (CV-8)

On October 26, 1942 during the Battle of the Santa Cruz Islands, the IJNAF
conducted the best coordinated and deadliest attack on a US Navy carrier
during the entire war. In an engagement lasting just 30 minutes, both D3A1
"Val" dive-bombers and B5N2 "Kate" torpedo-bombers targeted USS *Hornet*
(CV-8). The majority of the "Kates" were from *Zuikaku*, and they were led
into action by the IJNAF's most accomplished torpedo-bomber pilot, Lt Cdr
Shigeharu Murata. He had commanded the 40 B5N2s that had laid waste to
Battleship Row with their Type 91 torpedoes during the December 7, 1941
attack on Pearl Harbor. In this artwork, Murata leads his two wingmen toward
Hornet from the ship's starboard rear quarter. Against heavy fire, all three
aircraft dropped their Type 91s, two of which hit the carrier and led directly to
its loss. Murata did not survive the attack.

Previous Page

This remarkable photograph, taken on August 24, 1942, captures the moment
of detonation for the third 551lb bomb to hit USS *Enterprise* (CV-6) during
the Battle of the Eastern Solomons. This was a high-explosive weapon that
probably produced a low-order explosion, which, although spectacular,
resulted in only minor damage being inflicted on the carrier. The D3A1 that
dropped this bomb was shot down shortly after releasing its ordnance.
(NHHC)

CONTENTS

INTRODUCTION

The Pacific War was the first which was largely decided by air-to-sea combat. Aircraft attacking ships at sea used either bombs or torpedoes. In either case, the skill of the pilot was pivotal since he had to aim his aircraft at the target and maintain a constant course to improve his chances of scoring a hit. This final approach phase provided the best chance for antiaircraft fire to be effective. Hitting an attacking aircraft with antiaircraft fire often resulted in its destruction, but just making the attacker maneuver was an effective way to provide defense since it could spoil the pilot's aim.

During the Pacific War, high-level bombing was almost entirely ineffective. This forced medium bombers designed for high-level attacks to switch to low-level tactics, allowing torpedoes to be employed. When multi-engined bombers were used in this role, they tended to suffer very heavy losses. Dedicated torpedo- and dive-bombers were quickly determined to be more effective, resulting in them being the preferred aircraft types for such attacks for both the Imperial Japanese Naval Air Force (IJNAF) and the US Navy.

A dive-bomber could hit a maneuvering ship, and it was a far harder target for shipborne antiaircraft defenses to deal with than a medium bomber. A dive-bomber attacking at 300 knots from 12,000ft would reach its drop point in only 20 seconds. This made it challenging for antiaircraft defenses to react in time. Torpedo-bombing was dangerous for the attacking aircraft since they had to approach the target at low attitude and at low speed. But torpedoes were the only reliable way to sink large ships. The most effective method when targeting a ship was a combined attack by both dive-bombers and torpedo-bombers. This saturated its defenses and increased the likelihood of inflicting damage since the target could not maneuver to avoid all forms of attack at once.

At the beginning of the Pacific War, the Imperial Japanese Navy (IJN) had the most powerful naval air force in the world. Its ten aircraft carriers and 37 land-based air

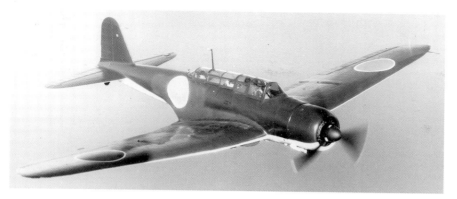

The Nakajima B5N Navy Type 97 Carrier Attack Bomber was the best torpedo-bomber in the world at the start of the Pacific War. Combined with the formidable Type 91 aerial torpedo, it gave the IJNAF an unsurpassed ship-killing capability. This particular B5N2, from the 931st Kokutai, was found at Saipan's Aslito airfield following the capture of the island in July 1944. It was returned to the United States and flight-evaluated, after which the aircraft was attached to a unit known as "The Navy's Flying Might" that toured the country taking part in nationwide Victory Loan promotions. (Navy History and Heritage Command – NHHC)

groups were equipped with 1,800 combat aircraft in total. In addition to its numerical superiority over the US Navy's carrier air groups, the IJNAF enjoyed a qualitative edge in both aircraft and aircrew training and experience.

Japanese war plans depended on the striking power of the IJN's air arm. Some 400 aircraft – the cream of the IJNAF – and their crews were embarked in carriers at the heart of the Pearl Harbor Attack Force, which was slated to open the conflict with a surprise attack on the US Navy's Pacific Fleet at its Pearl Harbor base in Hawaii. This was a supporting operation to the main Japanese offensive that was aimed at securing the vital resources of Southeast Asia. The campaign against US forces in the Philippines, the major concentration of British Commonwealth forces in Malaya, and the ill-defended Dutch East Indies was supported by three small aircraft carriers and just over 400 aircraft of the 11th Air Fleet assigned to the 21st, 22nd, and 23rd Air Flotillas.

During the inter-war period, the US Navy was aware of the potential threat posed by air attack. The nature of the threat posed by aircraft to ships at sea was constantly changing, and the Americans understood the importance the IJN attached to its naval air force. Nevertheless, in 1940, as the war in Europe raged, the US Navy was not fully ready to deal with a modern air threat due to years of inter-war budget austerity that had led to shortages in key equipment, especially light antiaircraft weapons.

Fortunately for the US Navy, it had the basis for quickly assembling a formidable system for fleet air defense. Friendly fighters were always seen as the best method of defeating enemy air attack, but these were not always available or suffered from poor direction when they were. Ships had to have the ability to defend themselves from air attack. Because of its pre-war design emphasis on shipboard air defense, the US Navy had already fitted the excellent 5in./38 dual-purpose gun and the world-class Mark (Mk) 37 fire control director on many ships. The excellent 20mm Oerlikon cannon was also coming into service, and the even better 40mm Bofors gun would soon follow. With the right doctrine and proper training, these tools would coalesce into a system that eventually gutted the finely-training pre-war IJNAF.

The outstanding antiaircraft weapon of 1942 was the US Navy's 20mm automatic cannon. In this photograph, taken during a gunnery exercise, the weapon is carried on a Mk 2 mounting with an adjustable trunnion height. The sailor on the far side of the gun controls the trunnion height with a large hand-wheel on the side of the mount. (NHHC)

CHRONOLOGY

1941

December 7 IJNAF carrier aircraft attack the bulk of the US Navy's Pacific Fleet in Pearl Harbor and sink or damage 18 ships.

December 10 IJNAF land-based G3M2 "Nell" and G4M1 "Betty" bombers sink the Royal Navy battleship HMS *Prince of Wales* and battlecruiser HMS *Repulse* in the South China Sea.

A D3A1 from the second wave to attack Pearl Harbor pulls out of its attack dive over a target, having just released its 551lb bomb. The aircraft has its dive brakes fully deployed. (NHHC)

1942

February 4 IJNAF land-based G3M2 "Nell" and G4M1 "Betty" bombers attack the Allied Combined Striking Force (CSF) and damage two US Navy cruisers.

February 15 IJNAF land-based G3M2 "Nell" and G4M1 "Betty" bombers attack the CSF and force it to abort its mission.

February 19 IJNAF carrier aircraft attack Darwin, in northern Australia, and sink eight ships including the destroyer USS *Peary* (DD-226).

February 20 Seventeen land-based IJNAF G4M1 "Betty" bombers engage the carrier USS *Lexington* (CV-2). Only two survive the attack and the carrier escapes unscathed.

April 5 IJNAF D3A1 "Vals" sink the Royal Navy heavy cruisers HMS *Cornwall* and HMS *Dorsetshire* off Ceylon.

April 9 HMS *Hermes* becomes the first carrier to be sunk by ship-based aircraft (D3A1 "Vals"), which also sink five other ships off Ceylon.

May 7 D3A1 "Vals" sink the US Navy oiler USS *Neosho* (AO-23) and the destroyer USS *Sims* (DD-409) in the Coral Sea. Thirty-one IJNAF land-based bombers inflict no damage on an American-Australian surface force.

May 8 In the Battle of the Coral Sea, Japanese carrier aircraft sink *Lexington* and damage USS *Yorktown* (CV-5).

June 4 In the Battle of Midway, IJNAF carrier aircraft sink *Yorktown*.

August 7	G4M1 "Betty" land-based bombers attack the US Navy invasion force off Guadalcanal but damage only a single destroyer.
August 8	Twenty-three G4M1 "Betty" land-based bombers attack the US Navy invasion force off Guadalcanal. Only five survive in exchange for badly damaging two ships, one of which, the destroyer USS *Jarvis* (DD-393), is finished off by G4M1s the following day.
August 24	In the Battle of the Eastern

Solomons, IJNAF carrier aircraft damage USS *Enterprise* (CV-6).

October 26 In the Battle of the Santa Cruz Islands, IJNAF carrier aircraft sink USS *Hornet* (CV-8) and damage *Enterprise*.

November 12 Nineteen G4M1 "Betty" land-based bombers attack a US convoy off Guadalcanal. Eleven bombers are lost, and the heavy cruiser USS *San Francisco* (CA-38) is the only ship to suffer any damage when it is struck by a crashing "Betty".

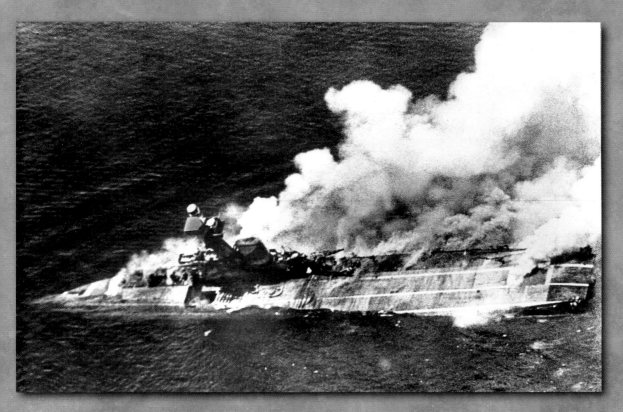

Hermes became the first carrier to be sunk by carrier-based dive-bombers on April 9, 1942, the Royal Navy warship quickly succumbing to multiple direct hits from D3A1s from *Shokaku*, *Zuikaku*, *Hiryu*, and *Akagi* while sailing off the coast of Ceylon. (Tony Holmes Collection)

DESIGN AND DEVELOPMENT

US NAVY ANTIAIRCRAFT CAPABILITIES

The US Navy had three basic types of antiaircraft weaponry in service during 1941–42. The first were long-range weapons, which included both 3in. and 5in. guns. These required extensive fire control systems to be effective. The second type consisted of intermediate weapons, which included 40mm guns in twin and quad mounts. These also required fire control directors to be effective. Finally, all US Navy ships mounted short-range weapons that consisted of 1.1in. quad mounts, 20mm Oerlikon guns, and 0.50in. machine guns. During this period the short-range weapons did not usually have fire control equipment beyond a ring sight and tracer rounds. Later in the war the US Navy provided them with a gyro sight, which greatly increased their effectiveness.

Defense of ships against air attack was dependent on the number of weapons carried, their effective ranges, and their accuracy. As the war progressed, the US Navy added as many antiaircraft guns as production and clear arcs of fire aboard ships allowed.

The Americans replaced the ineffective 0.50in. machine guns with 20mm guns, and 40mm cannon were introduced in the second half of 1942 aboard select ships. This weapon, especially in a quad mount, was very heavy, so only larger ships could take them. Production shortages meant there were never enough, resulting in the unsatisfactory 1.1in. quad mount being retained in service until the end of the war.

The 5in./38 caliber dual-purpose gun was the US Navy's standard long-range antiaircraft weapon throughout the war. This is a single mount photographed on board *Yorktown* in 1937. (NHHC)

The biggest challenge in shipboard antiaircraft gunnery was accuracy – getting rounds on or near a target which is changing in three dimensions from a platform that is also moving is very difficult to achieve. Fire control systems had to predict the location of the target when the shell arrived near it. A direct hit was very unlikely, so the fuse on the shell had to be set to detonate when it was within the closest possible distance of the target. This challenge was reduced with the arrival of Variable Time (VT) or proximity shells that would know when they were close to the target and explode. Only short-range antiaircraft guns were designed to actually hit the target, and this was made possible by the weapons' sheer volume of fire and the much-reduced range of the target.

In the event of conflict with Japan, the US Navy's pre-war plans called for the fleet to move through the Central Pacific to relieve the American garrison in the Philippines. Victory would be gained by the ensuing naval blockade of Japan. Since the Japanese held many islands in the Central and Western Pacific, this meant that the American fleet could potentially be subjected to a series of air attacks. To deal with this threat, the US Navy gave a high design priority to antiaircraft defense.

Battleships and heavy cruisers were modernized with new guns, 5in./25s replacing 3in./50s, and fitted with the Mk 19 fire control director. All destroyers starting with the Farragut-class were fitted with the 5in./38 dual-purpose gun and dedicated fire control systems. US Navy carriers, because of their importance, assessed vulnerability, and high likelihood to be a priority enemy target were best prepared for air attack. They were provided with either 5in./25 or 5in./38 dual purpose guns, paired with a complex fire control system, and an array of short-range weapons.

The US Navy closely followed the early wartime operations of the Royal Navy. The Luftwaffe's response to British warships during the ill-fated Norwegian campaign in April–June 1940 demonstrated a threat level from air attack that the US Navy was not prepared to counter. Its General Board was directed to study the problem of air defense and determine specific recommendations – its report was issued on May 25, 1940. The King Board (named after Rear Admiral Ernest King, later to be the US Navy's Chief of Naval Operations) stated that several active and passive measures needed to be carried out immediately.

It recommended that the 1.1in. quad mount be deployed on carriers, battleships, and heavy cruisers to protect against dive-bombers and low-level attack. Since production shortages of the new weapon existed, as an interim measure it was

Ships of TF 17 maneuver on October 26, 1942 during the Battle of the Santa Cruz Islands. This photograph shows a typical carrier formation of the early Pacific War period. *Hornet* is visible in the left-center, with either the heavy cruiser USS *Northampton* (CA-26) or USS *Pensacola* (CA-24) behind it. The antiaircraft cruisers USS *San Diego* (CL-53) and USS *Juneau* (CL-52) can be seen to the right, and four destroyers are also visible. (NHHC)

This view of the light cruiser USS *Honolulu* (CL-48) at Mare Island Navy Yard, California, on October 24, 1942 shows the US Navy's period antiaircraft weapons and fire control equipment. Along the ship's port side, two 5in./25 guns, two 20mm cannon, and a 1.1in. quad mount are visible. The Mk 51 director for the 1.1in. mount is circled in white at the base of the aft superstructure. Atop the superstructure is a Mk 34 director for the 5in./25 battery. (NHHC)

recommended that 3in./50 guns be fitted in their place. The 0.50in. machine guns were assessed as ineffective and their replacement with the new 20mm Oerlikon gun was envisioned. Passive measures included the provision of splinter protection for gun crews in the form of steel bulwarks. These measures were largely complete when the Pacific War began but were quickly determined to be inadequate in the face of the IJNAF's air onslaught.

Initial air defense tactics called for a succession of zone barrages that attacking aircraft would have to fly through. This tactic made sense at the time since the primary threat was assessed to be horizontal bombers. Torpedo-bombers were not considered a real threat and dive-bombing had not been developed. By 1936, the threat had changed, and the US Navy assessed that it had no "thoroughly effective defense" against dive-bombing. When target drones were introduced in 1939, results against this more realistic training device were universally bad. Firing exercises against a drone executing standard maneuvers demonstrated that even the best gun crews were unable to score a hit. When engaging high-flying drones representing level bombers, the volume of fire against such targets was judged to be insufficient.

Well before the war, the US Navy adopted a circular cruising disposition. This provided defense in depth, protection against attacks from any direction, and allowed the force to change directions easily. The circular formation was primarily for defense against air attack, but it was also suitable for steaming in waters known to be frequented by enemy submarines. When a gun action seemed inevitable, the heavy ships in the formation would change to a line-ahead formation.

Fleet air defense was much more effective if fighters were available for combat air patrol (CAP), and the advent of radar made this form of protection even more attractive. Effective fighter defense held the promise of destroying incoming enemy aircraft before they could attack. However, the art of fighter direction was in its infancy in 1942. In the four carrier battles that year, fighter direction varied from totally ineffective to moderately effective, but it never reached the point where it provided air-tight defense against enemy air attack. This forced the US Navy to continue its emphasis on antiaircraft defense.

The primary targets of Japanese air attacks in 1942 were American carriers. The US Navy debated before the war how to operate carriers. The key questions were whether carriers should operate together and how close they should be to the battle

line. The Pearl Harbor attack effectively removed the US Navy's battle line from the equation. When fast battleships arrived in the Pacific with the speed to operate with the carriers, they were integrated into the carrier task forces and used as heavy antiaircraft platforms. The more pressing question of whether carriers should operate together or dispersed was never fully decided in 1942. The pre-war notion that carriers were vulnerable to air attack drove the concept that they should operate separately so that they would avoid being detected and destroyed at once. Some carrier admirals preferred the benefit of operating carriers together to increase their offensive and defensive powers.

What happened in 1942 was that the US Navy usually operated its carriers in loose cooperation, with each 10–20 miles apart. This was done with the idea that they were

USS *North Carolina* (BB-55) photographed steaming off the US East Coast in April 1942. The ship carried an antiaircraft battery of 20 5in./38 guns in ten twin turrets, four 1.1in. quad mounts, 40 20mm single guns, and multiple 0.50in. machine guns that made it the most heavily armed antiaircraft platform in the world at the time. (NHHC)

far enough apart to escape detection by the same enemy scout aircraft, yet still close enough to operate together. In the event, neither proved to be true.

Fleet air defense was aided immensely by radar. Early warning was critical to get fighters airborne in time for an intercept and to send them in the right direction. Early war US Navy radars included the CXAM, CXAM-1, and the SC. The best of these was the CXAM-1, which could detect an aircraft formation flying at 10,000ft up to 70 miles away. However, early radars were unable to provide the exact height of incoming aircraft, which was a great handicap for effective fighter direction. Radar warning was usually sufficient to ensure that the ships of a task force were not surprised by enemy aircraft and that all guns were manned and ready.

Throughout 1942, the antiaircraft batteries on US Navy ships continued to grow. For example, at Coral Sea, *Yorktown* carried eight 5in./38 guns with directors, four 1.1in. quad mounts on local control, 24 20mm guns using tracers, and a few remaining 0.50in. machine guns. By October 1942 at the Battle of the Santa Cruz Islands, *Enterprise* retained the eight 5in./38 guns and four 1.1in. quad mounts, but had had its 20mm battery increased to 38 guns. In November, *Enterprise* had its 1.1in. mounts replaced by a new 40mm quad mount and the number of 20mm guns increased again to 48.

In June 1942 when the battleship USS *North Carolina* (BB-55) arrived in the Pacific, it embarked 20 5in./38 guns with two Mk 37 directors, four 1.1in. quad mounts, 40 20mm single mounts, and 28 0.50in. machine guns. Northampton-class heavy cruisers by early 1942 were fitted with eight 5in./25 guns, four 1.1in. quad mounts, and 14 20mm guns. The typical antiaircraft fit of destroyers employed on carrier escort duties was four or five 5in./38 single mounts and up to eight 20mm guns.

IJNAF CAPABILITIES AND ORGANIZATION

Each Japanese carrier had its own assigned air group. These were designed to be offensive instruments capable of out-ranging the enemy and gaining air dominance by quickly destroying the enemy's carriers. In accordance with this doctrine, carrier air groups were focused on attack aircraft at the expense of fighters. Air defense was a secondary mission, which meant that at the start of the war the numbers of fighters in an IJNAF carrier air group were inadequate to provide both fleet air defense and strike escort.

The IJNAF had two types of attack aircraft present in its carrier air groups. The first was what the Japanese called the carrier attack airplane, known in the US Navy as the torpedo-bomber. The second type was the dive-bomber, known to the Japanese as a carrier bomber. In the mid-1930s, the IJNAF favored carrier attack aircraft at the expense of dive-bombers. This proportion was linked to the Japanese fascination with the destructive power of torpedoes and the fact that dive-bombing was still in its formative stages in the IJNAF. By the late 1930s, the dive-bomber had demonstrated its potential, which led the Japanese to shift the composition of their carrier air groups to an equal proportion of attack aircraft and dive-bombers.

At the start of the Pacific War, most fleet carriers carried an equal number of carrier attack aircraft and dive-bombers – fighters accounted for the remaining third of the air group. Throughout 1942, the numbers of fighters gradually increased as air defense

OPPOSITE
This distinctively marked D3A1 was flown from *Zuikaku* during the December 1941–January 1942 period, the tail code "EII" and two white vertical stripes forward of the tail denoting its assignment to this particular carrier. The single horizontal tail stripe indicates that the aircraft was flown by a shotaicho, who led a tactical formation typically consisting of three dive-bombers. All aircraft assigned to carriers of the 1st Air Fleet had their tail markings applied in red. The D3A1 is armed with a 551lb bomb on its centerline.

D3A1 "VAL"

33ft 5in.

12ft 7in.

47ft 2in.

was shown to be a major weakness. The numbers of dive-bombers also grew since they were increasingly viewed as less vulnerable to enemy air defenses.

The original focus of Japanese carrier aircraft was scouting and spotting the fall of shot from their own battle line. By the end of the 1920s the doctrine for naval aircraft had begun to change, although it remained a defensive mindset. The use of fighters to cover the IJN's battle line and to gain control of the airspace over the enemy's battle line was emphasized. Such control was vital, since it denied the enemy intelligence from scouting and his ability to adjust fire from the air. The defensive focus of the IJNAF's carrier aircraft was mainly due to the inability of early attack aircraft to carry large payloads, which meant their ability to target heavily armored battleships was minimal.

This began to change in the 1930s with the arrival of better aircraft and weapons. As naval aviation became more offensively oriented, both the IJN and US Navy saw enemy carriers as the principal target. If such ships could be crippled, air dominance over the battle area was ensured. It was not necessary to sink opposing carriers – it was only necessary to wreck their flightdecks so that flight operations were rendered impossible. The Japanese believed that dive-bombing was the best way to accomplish this thanks to the precision associated with such attacks. When it came to sinking carriers, however, the IJNAF was convinced that torpedo-bombing was the answer. By the late 1930s the IJNAF had developed tactics to combine dive-bombing and torpedo-bombing in a single coordinated attack.

The IJNAF's original attempts to use aircraft in a maritime strike role focused on horizontal bombing by land-based types. Initially, the attacks were made from 7,000–16,000ft against stationary targets. When the Japanese decided to increase the realism of these bombing runs against moving targets, accuracy suffered. In response, bombing runs were conducted between 300 and 3,000ft at little more than 50 knots. This was an unrealistic attack profile that would have resulted in heavy losses to the attacking aircraft. In the mid-1930s bombing runs were moved to higher altitudes, but with larger numbers of aircraft to increase the bomb pattern in the hope of scoring at least some hits on a moving target. Nevertheless, the effectiveness of horizontal bombing was low, and remained so against moving targets until the start of the Pacific War.

The IJNAF was forced to look for more effective modes of air attack against naval targets. The first alternative tactic was torpedo-bombing. This found fertile ground in the IJNAF since the Japanese had long favored the use of the torpedo as it promised results even against large enemy warships and because it embraced the IJN's offensive spirit. Experimentation with airborne torpedo tactics began as early as 1916 but was hamstrung by technology. Early aircraft were too small to carry torpedoes, and early torpedoes often failed to successfully transition from being

The IJN emphasized torpedo combat, since only torpedoes had the power to sink large ships. This is the Type 91 aerial torpedo hit suffered by USS *Nevada* (BB-36) in the Pearl Harbor attack. The battleship's side armor is visible inside the hole's upper section. (NHHC)

U.S.S. NEVADA
PORT SIDE
2-19-42

air-dropped to making a true run in the water. Early torpedo exercises addressed this problem by dropping the fragile weapons from a height of only five to six feet at a speed of 50 knots. This may have allowed the torpedoes to successfully enter the water without damage, but it was a totally unrealistic combat attack profile.

Torpedo tactics became more viable with the development of better torpedoes and aircraft. In 1931, the Japanese developed the Type 91 aerial torpedo. This was a major step forward since it gave the IJN a weapon that could be launched at 100 knots from an altitude of up to 300ft. It was also fast – 42 knots – but had a relatively short range of 2,200 yards. The Japanese preferred a higher hit probability at shorter ranges at the expense of giving the Type 91 greater range so that the torpedo-bomber could use it as a stand-off weapon.

Precursor to the monoplane D3A, the Aichi D1A carrier bomber was closely based on the Heinkel He 66 dive-bomber, and almost 600 were delivered to the IJNAF during the mid-1930s. The aircraft would prove to be the mainstay of Japan's dive-bomber force in the Second Sino-Japanese conflict from 1937. Indeed, on December 12 that year, the US Navy river gunboat USS *Panay* (PR-5) was "erroneously" sunk by D1A2s while sailing on the Yangtze River. (Tony Holmes Collection)

The Type 91 remained in service throughout the Pacific War with some improvements. The size of the warhead was increased and the strength of the body structure improved, which allowed the launch speed to eventually increase to 350 knots in later versions. Among other adjustments, extensions to the torpedo's fins eventually solved the problem of getting the aerodynamics correct so that the torpedo entered the water and followed its pre-set course and depth. The result of all this effort was that the IJN started the war with the best aerial torpedo in the world. It would prove an essential element in the success the Japanese enjoyed against large warships early in the conflict.

Just as promising as torpedo attack was the tactic of dive-bombing. This was originally developed by the US Navy in the 1920s when fighter pilots experimented with diving almost vertically against naval targets. Using a near-vertical dive had many advantages and resulted in much greater accuracy even against smaller and faster ships. Using this tactic meant that the pilot did not have to correct for the horizontal motion of the aircraft – all he had to do was keep the target in sight during the dive. Since the attacks were conducted from altitude (12,000ft or more), and because of their steep dive angle and speed, dive-bombers were hard for the shipboard defenses to engage.

The Japanese embraced the concept of dive-bombing, although the fighters initially used were inadequate for the task. To conduct high-angle dive-bombing attacks, the Japanese had to develop a rugged aircraft designed specifically for dive-bombing. The firm of Aichi became the IJNAF's principal supplier of dive-bombers after its D1A Type 94 carrier bomber was ordered into production in 1934 – 590 were eventually built. The aircraft was essentially a locally-built Heinkel He 66 dive-bomber, which had been created in Germany following a request by Aichi. The D1A was replaced from 1939 by the much better-known Aichi D3A1 Type 99, this aircraft becoming famous during the Pacific War as the "Val" (its Allied reporting name from mid-1942).

The hardest thing for maritime attack aircraft to accomplish was to hit a moving target using horizontal bombing. The Japanese recognized the difficulty in this tactic,

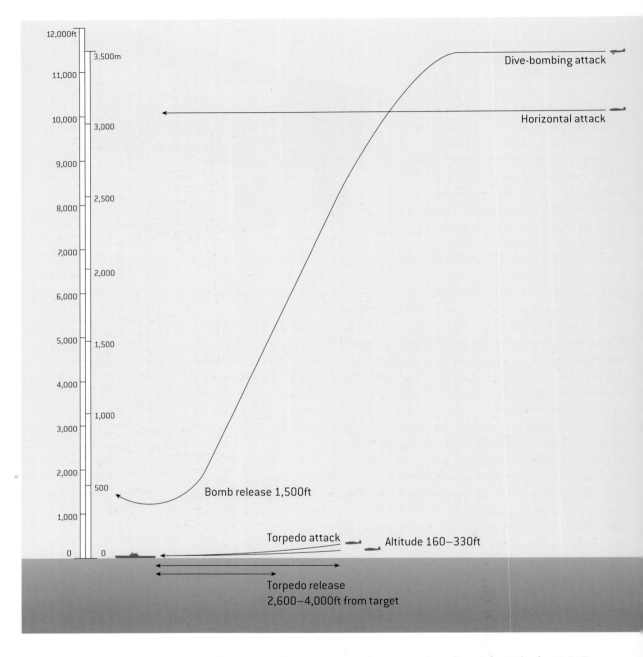

The following are the labels within the figure:

12,000ft

3,500m

Dive-bombing attack

Horizontal attack

Bomb release 1,500ft

Torpedo attack   Altitude 160–330ft

Torpedo release
2,600–4,000ft from target

IJNAF horizontal, dive- and torpedo-bombing attack profiles against US Navy ships.

and despite intensive practice results remained mediocre. In 1941 the IJNAF was so discouraged with the seemingly ineffective tactic that it considered abandoning it to concentrate on torpedo- and dive-bombing.

At the same time planning for the Pearl Harbor operation was ramping up, and horizontal bombing was resurrected as the only way to hit the US Navy's capital ships moored inboard in groups of two along Ford Island's Battleship Row. The ships moored outboard were vulnerable to torpedo attack, and while the ships inboard could be hit by dive-bombers, these aircraft carried only 551lb bombs that did not have the penetrative

16

power to pierce battleship armor. However, it was calculated that a carrier attack aircraft's solitary 1,764lb bomb could penetrate the horizontal armor of US Navy battleships.

The IJNAF solved the issues previously associated with horizontal bombing as follows. Firstly, it addressed the problem of unequal skill levels between pilots and their bombardiers. Being a pilot was a prestigious outcome following flight training, while few high-quality graduates chose to become bombardiers. Cross-training some pilots as bombardiers fixed this issue. The IJNAF also reduced the doctrinal altitude of horizontal bombing from 13,000ft down to 10,000ft. This improved accuracy, while still providing the needed penetrative power to punch through battleship armor. It did, however, make the bomber more vulnerable to antiaircraft fire. The final adjustment was to break the carrier attack aircraft up into groups of five that dropped their bombs simultaneously upon a signal from the lead bombardier.

For the Pearl Harbor operation, the IJNAF developed a special bomb from a 16in. shell which was modified to explode after penetration, instead of upon contact. Against stationary targets, and with the benefit of intensive training, the IJNAF carrier attack aircraft crews achieved impressive results in the summer of 1941 as they prepared for the Pearl Harbor strike. IJNAF long-range bomber units also adopted the same tactics, although they used the normal 1,764lb bomb instead of the modified battleship shells that were reserved for the Pearl Harbor operation.

The success of horizontal bombing was highly dependent on the skill of the pilot and bombardier. After some spectacular results early in the war, the effectiveness of horizontal bombing drastically declined due to heavy aircrew losses and improved American air defenses.

The IJNAF expected much better results from dive-bombing. In 1940–41, the Japanese refined the art of dive-bombing led by Lt Sadamu Takahashi, who graduated from flight training in 1935 and had extensive experience in both land- and carrier-based dive-bomber units. The tactic that he perfected called for the dive-bomber to approach the target head-on at some 10,000ft about 23–35 miles from the target. The head-on approach was preferred, but in some cases a stern attack was the best tactical solution. Attacking along the length of the target gave a much better chance of success,

The arrival of the Nakajima B5N1 carrier attack aircraft allowed the IJNAF to refine its tactics for the employment of what it saw as the key weapon in the future fight against the Pacific Fleet – the Type 91 torpedo. This example, from the Yokosuka Kokutai (the backward katakana symbol "ヨ" – looking like a backward "E" – in the B5N1's tail code translates to "YO" for "Yokosuka"), has bomb racks fitted, however. The aircraft could also be used as a level bomber. (Philip Jarrett Collection)

rather than from the target's beam. If the wind was greater than 30 knots, the preferred approach was made keeping the wind at the tail of the dive-bombers to reduce wind drift. If several dive-bomber units were involved in the same attack, the attack was conducted from several different angles.

The dive-bombers formed an echelon formation, went to full throttle, and began a ten-degree dive. When the lead pilot judged the formation was close enough, he would begin a 65-degree dive and aim for a point where the target's course and speed would take it. The bomb was released at about 2,000ft above the target. Each aircraft would attack in order. After bomb release, the dive-bombers would open their dive brakes, pull out of the dive and exit the area at low altitude at maximum speed.

During the war, the IJNAF assessed that a typical 18-aircraft dive-bomber squadron would be effective, but suffer heavy losses in the process. In 1942, the practice was adopted that some aircraft would carry high-explosive bombs to suppress the target's antiaircraft fire. Of the 18 attacking aircraft, the Japanese expected that five or six would score hits and eight would be shot down. Unlike most Japanese pre-war assessments regarding the effectiveness of their tactics, this assessment turned out to be essentially correct.

With the Nakajima B5N1 carrier attack aircraft and the Type 91 torpedo, the IJNAF was able to refine its torpedo attack tactics in the years leading up to the start of the war. By 1937, it was normal to release the Type 91 at heights of up to 660ft and at speeds of up to 120 knots. The usual distance from the target when the torpedo was released was 3,300ft. This was much better than the drop heights used by the US Navy and Royal Navy, but it still meant torpedo-bombers were approaching a heavily defended target at low altitudes and slow speeds. The IJNAF expected losses to be heavy, and that combat results would be one-third of those recorded in peacetime exercises.

By the start of the Pacific War torpedo attack tactics had been settled but concerns about heavy losses remained. The torpedo-bombers preferred to approach the target head-on from an altitude of between 3,300–9,800ft, with aircraft going into a dive to gain speed some 12–14 miles from the target. At this point, the torpedo-bombers divided up to engage the target from both sides. This was known as a "hammer and anvil" attack, and it was designed to catch the target broadside no matter which way it turned. The attacking aircraft approached the target in a loose string formation, or if the antiaircraft fire was intense, in a line abreast formation. Torpedoes were dropped from an altitude of 160–330ft at a speed of 140–162 knots. The distance from the target was typically 2,600–4,000ft.

In addition to devoting much effort to perfecting the individual forms of attack, the IJNAF also gave priority to coordinating these attacks into a single operation. The thinking went that it might be possible for the enemy to defend against either dive-bombing or torpedo attacks, but if these were conducted closely together then enemy defenses would be overwhelmed. In such an operation, fighters would sweep the airspace over the target of its defending CAP and then strafe the enemy carriers. These were immediately followed by dive-bombers and then torpedo-bombers. Such a closely sequenced attack was very difficult to achieve, since it required precision timing and favorable tactical circumstances. Only the most skilled and aggressive aircrews had a chance of pulling such an attack off, and only under the direction of a bold leader.

TECHNICAL SPECIFICATIONS

US NAVY SHIPBOARD ANTIAIRCRAFT WEAPONS

Larger US Navy ships carried three types of antiaircraft weapons. The longest-range guns were of a medium caliber and were epitomized by the 5in./38 dual-purpose gun. Intermediate-range weapons (the 40mm gun) provided the next layer of defense. Every ship carried the largest possible number of short-range weapons, most often the 20mm gun, to provide close-in defense.

Principal US Navy Antiaircraft Guns				
Weapon	Muzzle velocity (ft/sec)	Ceiling (ft)	Shell weight (lbs)	Rate of fire (rounds per minute, theoretical)
5in./25	2,110	27,400	52	14
5in./38	2,600	37,200	54	15–20
40mm	2,890	22,800	2	160
1.1in. Mk 1/1	2,700	19,000	0.92	140
20mm	2,740	10,000	0.27	450

The 5in./25 gun's design dated back to early 1921 and it was installed on older cruisers, battleships and carriers. Although the weapon, which had a short barrel to make it easier to engage fast targets, was created as a dual-purpose gun, its low velocity did not give it the flat trajectory needed to engage surface targets. The 5in./38 was the follow-on to the 5in./25. This was a very successful design, and it became the US Navy's standard dual-purpose gun of World War II. Indeed, it is generally considered to be the most successful gun of its type ever built. The weapon's longer barrel increased muzzle velocity and thus ceiling against aircraft. Firing semi-fixed ammunition, the hand-operated but power-rammed gun achieved a high rate of fire – a well-trained crew could fire 15 rounds per minute or more.

Older ships carried the 5in./25 weapon in single mounts. This crew is conducting gunnery drills on board the heavy cruiser USS *Astoria* (CA-34) in spring 1942. (NHHC)

The rise of the dive-bomber pushed the US Navy to develop short-ranged weapons. The standard American antiaircraft machine gun before the war was the water-cooled 0.50in. weapon. Each battleship and heavy cruiser boasted eight such guns, and destroyers had four. Carriers carried a larger but variable number. The only guidance system for the operator was tracer rounds. It was apparent early in the war that the weapon was obsolete in an antiaircraft role, primarily

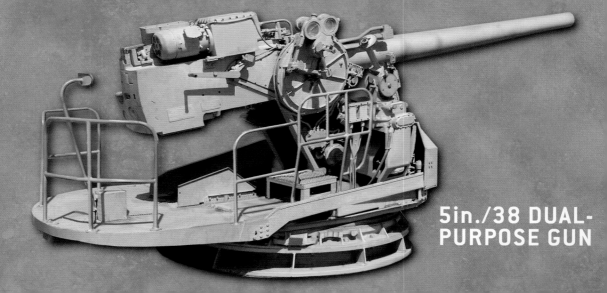

The US Navy's standard long-range medium caliber antiaircraft weapon at the start of the Pacific War was the 5in./38 dual-purpose gun. Based on the 5in./25 weapon of the early 1930s, the 5.in/38 had a longer barrel for increased muzzle velocity and thus ceiling against aircraft.

Firing semi-fixed ammunition, the hand-operated but power-rammed gun could achieve a high rate of fire. Indeed, a well-trained crew could fire 15 rounds per minute or more. The 5.in/38 is generally considered to be the most successful gun of its type ever built.

5in./38 DUAL-PURPOSE GUN

because of its lack of hitting power. The 0.50in. gun was replaced as soon as possible by the 20mm Oerlikon cannon.

Complementing the 0.50in. machine gun was the 1.1in. machine cannon. Development of this weapon commenced in 1928, its explosive 1lb shell being deemed to be much more effective than the non-exploding machine gun round. Furthermore, the four barrels of the quad mount gave the desired volume of fire necessary to down an aircraft. The first mount was not completed until 1935, and it was rushed into production so that the inadequate 0.50in. weapon could be replaced as soon as possible. Production ended in December 1942 with 832 units after deliveries of the much superior 40mm Bofors gun ramped up. The 1.1in. machine cannon was hated by gunnery crews because of its propensity to jam.

The US Navy's standard short-range antiaircraft weapon for the entire war was the Swiss-designed 20mm Oerlikon gun. Very reliable, it enjoyed a high reputation with American gunners throughout the war. The weapon was air-cooled, fairly lightweight, and the early mountings required no external power source. This allowed it to be fitted in large numbers on destroyers, cruisers, battleships and carriers wherever there was a clear arc of fire. Although the gun's small 20mm round proved unable to handle the kamikaze threat in the final ten months of the

This 1.1in. quad mount was photographed on board the battleship USS *Pennsylvania* (BB-38) in February 1942. The weapon suffered from reliability issues and fired a small shell, and was replaced by the 40mm quad mount from late 1942. (NHHC)

20mm OERLIKON

The US Navy's standard short-range antiaircraft weapon for the entire war was the Swiss-designed 20mm Oerlikon gun. Its reliability in combat in the Pacific quickly drew praise from American gunners, and it remained a favorite with them through to war's end.

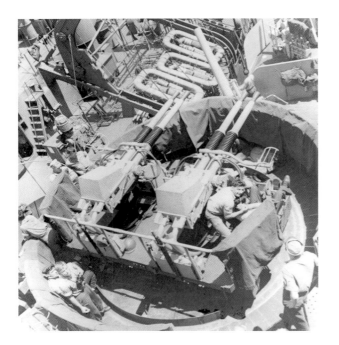

The iconic antiaircraft gun of the Pacific War was the quad 40mm Bofors mount. However, this weapon was not introduced until late 1942, and it therefore played only a small role in the carrier battles of that year. This view was taken on board the USS *Portland* (CA-33) in 1944. (NHHC)

war in the Pacific, in 1942 the 20mm Oerlikon cannon was a mainstay of US Navy shipborne antiaircraft defenses.

The Swedish-designed 40mm Bofors gun made its debut at the Battle of the Santa Cruz Islands in October 1942. It eventually replaced the 1.1in. quad mount and was used aboard larger US Navy ships in dual and quad mounts. It became the favored antiaircraft weapon later in the war when the kamikaze threat was paramount.

US NAVY FIRE CONTROL SYSTEMS

The US Navy's first long-range fire control system was the Mk 19. It was comprised of a director, aimed at the target, and two "altiscopes" that acted as range and height-finders and which were also directed at the target. With the data generated, elevation and azimuth information were provided to the guns, as were fusing directions for the shells. The Mk 19 was obsolete well before the war, but funds were not available to replace it. The US Navy was forced to opt for an evolutionary approach to keep its fire control equipment effective. In the case of the Mk 19, it was combined with a stereo rangefinder in a single enclosed mount and called the Director Mount Mk 1. This equipped battleships and heavy cruisers before the war.

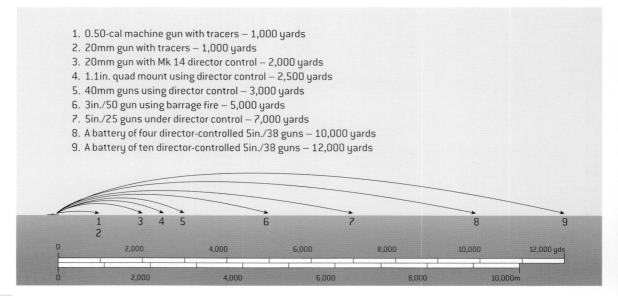

1. 0.50-cal machine gun with tracers – 1,000 yards
2. 20mm gun with tracers – 1,000 yards
3. 20mm gun with Mk 14 director control – 2,000 yards
4. 1.1in. quad mount using director control – 2,500 yards
5. 40mm guns using director control – 3,000 yards
6. 3in./50 gun using barrage fire – 5,000 yards
7. 5in./25 guns under director control – 7,000 yards
8. A battery of four director-controlled 5in./38 guns – 10,000 yards
9. A battery of ten director-controlled 5in./38 guns – 12,000 yards

The US Navy improved the Mk 19 into the Mks 28 and 33 with the adoption of stereo rangefinders into a single integrated director. The Mk 28 appeared in 1933 and was fitted on the modernized New Mexico-class battleships and the first five New Orleans-class heavy cruisers. It could handle a target flying at up to 220 knots but lacked a power drive.

The Mk 28 was modified into the Mk 33, which was the first director designed to handle the new 5in./38 gun. The Mk 33 was the main pre-war long-range director, and it was fitted to the carriers USS *Ranger* (CV-4), *Yorktown*, *Enterprise*, and USS *Wasp* (CV-7), Portland- and Brooklyn-class cruisers, later New Orleans-class cruisers, and all new classes of destroyers with 5in./38 turrets up to the Sims-class. The Mk 33 was self-contained with its own rangefinder. It had power drive, which helped with tracking against faster targets and in keeping the mount stabilized – critically important on small ships like destroyers.

This is a Mk 37 fire control director, complete with victory markings for Japanese aircraft destroyed, aboard a destroyer in 1944. Its effectiveness has been increased with the addition of a Mk 4 Fire Control Radar, mounted atop the Mk 37's turret. This was the standard director for the 5in./38 gun. (NHHC)

The Mk 33 could handle targets flying at speeds up to 320 knots, and it had a special mode to track diving targets traveling at up to 400 knots. Although early combat experience in the Pacific revealed that the Mk 33 was too slow to generate target solutions, especially against a maneuvering aircraft, it served until the end of the war.

The Mk 37 was the best long-range fire control director of the war. Its computer was moved below decks and was connected automatically with the director. The fuse-setting system was placed in the ammunition hoist, which provided better control. This was the standard medium-range fire control system employed on all US Navy ships constructed during World War II. The Mk 37 could automatically generate solutions on targets moving at 400 knots horizontally and 250 knots diving.

The effectiveness of the system was enhanced with the integration of radar. The first radar to be incorporated was the Mk 4, which reduced the time required to generate a target solution. Most Mk 37 directors were equipped with radar by October 1942. The Mk 37 did have weaknesses. It was best beyond 6,000 yards and was increasingly less accurate down to 3,000 yards and very inaccurate closer than 300 yards. It replaced the Mk 33 system on *Enterprise*, and was fitted on the heavy cruisers USS *Vincennes* (CA-44) and USS *Wichita* (CA-45) and the last three Brooklyn-class light cruisers. All modern battleships, Essex-class carriers, and wartime cruiser and destroyer construction received the Mk 37 director, with large ships carrying two.

The US Navy had problems getting enough directors for the growing numbers of medium and light antiaircraft guns fitted on combatants. The pre-war family of directors quickly proved too complex or ineffective, or both, once in combat. The answer came out of desperation when a very simple, single-man director was developed. This became the Mk 51, and it was readily mass-produced in sufficient quantities to provide direction for the growing number of 40mm mounts. The Mk 51 was

OPPOSITE

Based on the first year of the Pacific War, this is how the US Navy assessed the effective ranges of its principal antiaircraft weapons.

Mk 51 DIRECTOR

Faced with a shortage of complex fire control directors for its ever-increasing fleet of ships, the US Navy created the simple, single-man Mk 51 director for the control of medium and light antiaircraft guns being fitted in larger numbers on combatants. Readily mass-produced in sufficient quantities to provide direction for the growing number of 40mm mounts, as well as existing 1.1in. quad mounts, the Mk 51 was essentially a Mk 14 gyro sight on a pedestal. Thanks to its placement away from the vibration, smoke, and flash of a gun being fired, the Mk 51 proved to be much more effective than preceding directors.

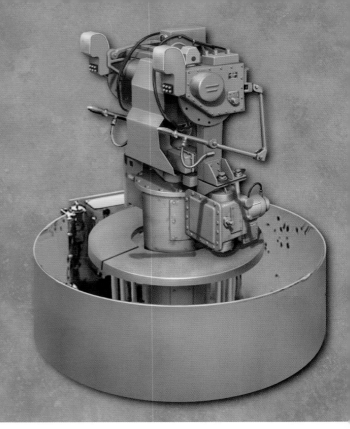

essentially a Mk 14 gyro sight on a pedestal. Because it was placed away from the vibration, smoke and flash of a gun being fired, it was much more effective. The Mk 51 was hand-slewed, so the director could respond to surprise attacks. It provided training and elevation commands to the mount, which were then executed by electric power.

The 1.1in. quad mount used the Mk 44 for guidance, although this was only an interim solution and just 85 were made. Some were modified to control the 40mm mounts before the arrival of the Mk 51. Guidance for the 20mm cannon was simpler. Through 1942, the only guidance system for gunners was to track the fall of shot through tracer rounds and ring sights, the latter being calibrated for targets moving at different speeds. The 20mm mounts were soon fitted with Mk 14 gyro-sights, which the US Navy estimated to be 50 per cent more effective than the ring sight and tracers method. The Mk 14 was designed to handle a 200-knot target, but it proved reasonably accurate against aircraft flying at 500 knots.

IJNAF MARITIME ATTACK AIRCRAFT

The first manifestation of the IJNAF's desire to conduct long-range maritime strike missions was the Mitsubishi G3M Navy Type 96 Attack Bomber. At the behest of Rear Admiral Isoroku Yamamoto, then head of the IJN's Aeronautics Department, Mitsubishi was given a non-competitive contract to start development of a twin-engined long-range reconnaissance aircraft. This machine first flew in 1934 and was a very successful design. This spurred the IJN to award Mitsubishi another non-competitive contract to develop a bomber able to carry a 1,764lb payload, which was the weight of the IJNAF's standard air-launched torpedo. Work progressed quickly and the first prototype flew in July 1935.

Construction of the production version, the Navy Type 96 Attack Bomber Model 11 (G3M1), began in June 1936. It was quickly replaced by the G3M2 Model 21, which was fitted with more powerful engines and could carry slightly more fuel. A total of 343 aircraft were built. Mitsubishi then switched to the G3M2 Model 22, which had a greater defensive armament following lessons learned in combat over China – the Model 21's principal weakness had been its paucity of defensive weaponry. Mitsubishi built 238 Model 22s through to 1941. Nakajima continued production of the aircraft into 1943, building 412 G3M3 Model 23s that featured more powerful engines and an increased fuel capacity. The G3M was later given the Allied reporting name "Nell".

The IJNAF's first land-based medium bomber was the Mitsubishi G3M Navy Type 96 Attack Bomber, which gave the Japanese a capable long-range offensive platform. These examples are G3M2 Model 22s, capable of carrying up to 1,764lb of bombs or a single Mk 91 torpedo of an identical weight. (Philip Jarrett Collection)

G3M2 Type 96 Model 22 Specification

Powerplant	Two 1,075hp Mitsubishi Kinsei 41 or 42 radial engines
Dimensions	
Span	82ft 0.25in.
Length	53ft 12in.
Height	12ft 1in.
Wing area	807 sq ft
Weights	
Empty	10,936lb
Loaded	17,637lb
Performance	
Max speed	232mph at 13,715ft
Range	2,730 miles
Ceiling	29,950ft
Payload	One Type 91 torpedo or 1,764lb of bombs carried externally
Armament	Four 7.7mm Type 92 machine guns and one 20mm Type 99-1 cannon

Although the G3M was considered a successful aircraft, the IJNAF desired a bomber with greater speed and range. Mitsubishi began design work on an improved bomber in September 1937, and commenced flight testing in October 1939. The new bomber, designated the Mitsubishi G4M Navy Type 1 Attack Bomber, was a remarkable aircraft.

During testing the prototype exceeded requirements by recording a top speed of 276mph and a range of 3,450 miles. Production of the Navy Type 1 Attack Bomber Model 11 was authorized in 1940, and by the following summer the aircraft was employed in combat operations over China. The Model 12 entered service in 1942 with improved engines and limited protection for the wing and fuselage fuel tanks – the latter were also fitted with fire-extinguishing systems. This increased weight, which slightly decreased speed and range.

G4M1 Navy Type 1 Attack Bombers of the Kanoya Kokutai fly in tight formation during the "Southern Advance" in early 1942. Considered to be the IJNAF's best land-based torpedo bomber group at the start of the Pacific War, the Kanoya Kokutai helped to destroy Force Z in the South China Sea on December 10, 1941. This proved to be the high point for the IJNAF's land-based bomber units. (NHHC)

The G4M was a brilliant design that fulfilled the IJNAF's requirement for immense range as part of its offensive strategy. However, this was achieved at the expense of protection. When facing minimal fighter resistance, as was the case early in the war, this vulnerability was not exposed. However, when engaged by better armed fighters, the result was heavy losses. The Model 11 had no armor or fuel tank protection, and the Model 12 had only a limited ability to absorb combat damage. Nevertheless, the G4M remained in service throughout the war despite an inevitable increase in losses to enemy fighters. The Allied reporting name for the G4M was "Betty".

G4M1 Type 1 Model 11 Specification

Powerplant	Two 1,530hp Mitsubishi Mk 4a Kasei 11 radial engines
Dimensions	
Span	82ft 0.25in.
Length	65ft 7in.
Height	19ft 8in.
Wing area	841 sq ft
Weights	
Empty	14,991lb
Loaded	20,944lb
Performance	
Max speed	266mph at 13,780ft
Range	3,750 miles
Ceiling	29,365ft (Model 12)
Payload	One Type 91 torpedo or 1,764lb of bombs carried internally
Armament	Four 7.7mm Type 92 machine guns and one 20mm Type 99-1 cannon

OPPOSITE

This aircraft, from the 4th Kokutai on Rabaul, participated in the disastrous mission against the carrier *Lexington* on February 20, 1942. Commanded by Lt Cdr Takuzo Ito, the bomber was immortalized in a famous photographic sequence taken from the carrier during its attempted suicide dive on the ship. Formerly assigned to the Takeo Kokutai, the G4M1 was marked with two horizontal tail stripes to denote its chutai (sub-group) affiliation within the 4th Kokutai (air group). The "F" in "F-348" was the unit code letter assigned to the kokutai.

In addition to its land-based long-range bombers, the IJNAF also operated several types of carrier-based aircraft. All Japanese fleet carriers carried a single squadron of dive-bombers and a single squadron of attack aircraft, with the latter being able to perform both the torpedo-bomber or level bomber roles.

G4M1 TYPE 1 MODEL 11

65ft 7in.

19ft 8in.

82ft 0.25in.

F-348

Armed with a Type 98 No. 25 532lb land-attack bomb with a HE fuse, this B5N2 was assigned to *Hiryu* during the Pearl Harbor operation – although this photograph was taken either before or after the raid. *Hiryu's* B5N2s performed both level-bombing and torpedo attacks on Battleship Row. Those B5N2s not equipped with torpedoes targeted the US Navy capital ships with a single Type 99 No. 80 Mk 5 1,764lb armor-piercing bomb. (Tony Holmes Collection)

Perhaps the key IJNAF carrier-based strike aircraft at the start of the war was the Nakajima B5N Navy Type 97 Carrier Attack Bomber (later given the Allied reporting name of "Kate"), which, at the time, was the most modern torpedo-bomber in the world. It gave the IJNAF the ship-killing power to sink any US Navy warship. The IJN had issued its requirement for a new attack bomber in 1935, and Nakajima's prototype first flew in January 1937. After some modification, the Nakajima entrant secured a contract and went into production in November 1937. The version that became famous in the Pacific War first flew in December 1939 and entered production as the B5N2 Navy Type 97 Carrier Bomber Model 12. It featured a more powerful and reliable engine, but little increase in speed over the original B5N1.

With its fairly high top speed and reliable Type 91 aerial torpedo, the B5N2 proved a formidable ship-killer. However, its effectiveness declined throughout 1942 as Allied ship-borne and aerial defenses took an increasing toll of these aircraft. Even in the face of improving US Navy air defenses, the B5N2 was a deadly weapon when crewed by skilled aviators. The aircraft's weaknesses meant its days as a frontline aircraft were

B5N2 Type 97 Model 12 Specifications	
Engine	1,000hp Nakajima NK 1B Sakae 11 radial engine
Dimensions	
Span	50ft 11in.
Length	33ft 10in.
Height	12ft 2in.
Wing area	406 sq ft
Weights	
Empty	5,024lb
Loaded	8,378lb
Performance	
Max speed	235mph at 11,810ft
Range	1,240 miles
Ceiling	27,100ft
Payload	Type 91 torpedo or 1,764lb of bombs
Armament	One 7.7mm Type 92 rear-firing machine gun

numbered by the fall of 1942, its principal vulnerability being a lack of protection for the crew and the fuel tank. Additionally, the B5N2 had only a single defensive machine gun fitted in the rear of the cockpit.

The standard dive-bomber going into the war, and for most of 1942, was the Aichi D3A1 Navy Type 99 Carrier Bomber Model 11. In response to an IJN requirement issued in 1936, Aichi began development of an improved dive-bomber to replace its D1A2 then in service. When flight testing of the new aircraft began in December 1937, it revealed significant problems. After modifications, Aichi was awarded the contract for the IJNAF's new dive-bomber in December 1939. The Model 11 was a superb dive-bombing platform and was also very maneuverable. In fall 1942, the D3A2 Model 22 began to enter service. This version had a more powerful engine and carried additional fuel.

The D3A was undeniably successful. In fact, it sank more Allied ships than any other Japanese aircraft when used in a conventional role. This was due to the fact that the dive-bomber encountered minimal Allied fighter opposition early in the war, and

The IJNAF's standard carrier-based dive-bomber was the Aichi D3A1 Navy Type 99 Carrier Bomber. The pilot of this example, carrying a single 551lb ordinary bomb on its centreline, has opened the throttle, allowing the dive-bomber to gain speed as it accelerates along *Kaga*'s flightdeck at 0715 hrs. This aircraft participated in the second wave strike on Pearl Harbor on December 7, 1941.
(Tony Holmes Collection)

D3A1 Type 99 Model 11 Specifications

Engine	1,000hp Mitsubishi Kinsei 43 radial engine
Dimensions	
Span	47ft 2in.
Length	33ft 5in.
Height	12ft 7in.
Wing area	375 sq ft
Weights	
Empty	5,309lb
Loaded	8,047lb
Performance	
Max speed	240 mph at 9,845ft
Range	915 miles
Ceiling	30,050ft
Payload	One 551lb bomb or two 132lb bombs
Armament	Two 7.7mm Type 97 machine guns forward and one 7.7mm Type 92 rear-firing machine gun

TYPE 91 MOD 2 TORPEDO

Weighing 1,841lb, the Type 91 Mod 2 Airborne Torpedo was the most effective weapon of its type at the start of the Pacific War. Fitted with a 452lb warhead and capable of traveling at 42 knots for up to 2,000 yards, it proved to be both reliable and deadly when employed by the B5N2 at Pearl Harbor and during the subsequent carrier battles of 1942. Indeed, it gave IJNAF air groups an effective ship-killing power not possessed by US Navy carrier aircraft. Note the wooden fins on the torpedo that were fitted to ensure it made the proper transition from being air dropped to running at its correct depth.

because it was crewed by skilled aviators. The D3A's performance was mediocre, with a slow top speed, and it was restricted to carrying only a single 551lb bomb. The aircraft also proved unable to withstand substantial battle damage.

TYPE 91 TORPEDO

The IJNAF had the immense benefit of having a reliable air-launched torpedo in operational service at the start of the war. This was the Type 91, dating from 1931. The Mod 2 of this weapon was introduced in April 1941 and carried a larger warhead, among other modifications. In October 1941 the Mod 3 was introduced, but it does not seem to have entered service until late 1942. This version was also fitted with a larger warhead.

Type 91 Mod 2 Airborne Torpedo Specification	
Dimensions	
Diameter	17.7in.
Length	18ft
Weight	1,841lb
Warhead	452lb
Speed	41–43 knots
Range	2,200 yards

IJNAF BOMBS

The normal ship attack bomb load-out for IJNAF dive-bombers was one semi-armor piercing (SAP) Type 99 No. 25 551lb common bomb. In 1942, the Japanese devised a tactic in which one dive-bomber out of three carried a Type 98

TYPE 99 No 25 551LB BOMB

The semi-armor piercing Type 99 No. 25 551lb common bomb was one of the principal weapons carried by IJNAF maritime attack aircraft. The body of the bomb consisted of one piece of machined-forged steel three-quarters of an inch in thickness. It was threaded in the nose to receive a fuse. The after end of the body was threaded internally to accommodate a male base plate. The latter was drilled centrally to receive the tail fuse. The weapon's tail cone was secured to the base plate by six screws. Four fins were welded to the tail cone and braced by a single set of box-type struts. The bomb body was filled with Type 91 (trinitroanisol) explosive. Designed in 1938 and adopted by the IJNAF the following year, the Type 99 No. 25 common bomb was capable of penetrating two inches of armor before exploding.

No. 25 532lb land-attack bomb with a high explosive warhead (HE) fused for instantaneous detonation. The idea was that the HE-equipped bomber would attack first and that its bomb would wreak havoc on the target's unprotected antiaircraft guns and crews. This suppression would make the approach of the aircraft carrying the SAP bombs easier.

The IJNAF's carrier attack aircraft and land-based bombers carried the same weapons as the dive-bombers, but in addition could carry much-larger 1,760lb bombs. These came in two varieties. The Type 99 Model 80-3 was specially designed for the Pearl Harbor attack. It used a 16in. battleship shell to provide the mass and penetrating power to punch through the horizontal armor of US Navy battleships. The Type 80 1,760lb land-attack bomb was also used against ships. Finally, all IJNAF maritime attack aircraft could carry general-purpose 132lb bombs.

The Type 91 Mod 2 Airborne Torpedo was the outstanding aerial torpedo of the Pacific War, and it was the main weapon responsible for sinking three US Navy carriers in 1942. Fitted with a 520lb warhead, the Type 91 was capable of traveling at up to 43 knots for 2,200 yards. (NHHC)

THE STRATEGIC SITUATION

At the start of the Pacific War, the IJN was in the process of changing its Battle Instructions. Those in effect when the conflict commenced placed the battleship at the core of the fleet and as the final arbiter of victory in the elaborate set-piece battle that the IJN had trained to fight. Within this framework, the Japanese clearly understood the importance of naval air power. Going into the war it was the IJN's one clear area of advantage, since the inter-war naval treaties had imposed numerical inferiority against the US Navy in all types of warships. Furthermore, the US Navy was backed by an immense industrial advantage which meant that the IJN would be perpetually outnumbered.

In an effort to compensate for this, the IJN stressed high levels of training for all fleet components and the ability to hit the enemy at ranges from which he could not respond effectively. For the IJNAF, existing doctrine was offensively oriented. The target priority had shifted from attacking enemy battleships to attacking carriers. Gaining air superiority was essential before the decisive phase of combat began between surface forces. To gain air superiority, the enemy carriers were to be attacked pre-emptively and from long range. The employment of both land-based and carrier-based aviation was necessary for victory.

Prior to the war, the IJN also struggled with the issue of whether to disperse or concentrate its carriers. Since the latter were thought to be extremely vulnerable when attacked, dispersal seemed to increase the prospects of survival, as it meant that only a portion of friendly carriers could be detected and attacked. The proponents of concentration eventually carried the day by making the case that massed carriers offered considerably more offensive power, including better prospects for coordinating attacks, and that their defensive powers were also increased since they could mass fighter protection and antiaircraft fire. During 1941–42 this translated into two or three carrier divisions operating together in a box formation.

There were problems in adopting this new doctrine, however. Previously, carriers operated together in divisions in a semi-independent but strictly adjunct role to the fleet they were assigned to. Both the aviation advocates and the big-gun admirals were content with this arrangement. In 1940, a few aviation advocates began to press the Commander of the Combined Fleet, Adm Isoruku Yamamoto, to concentrate the existing carrier divisions into a single command to form an "air fleet" that could train and fight together. Not until December 1940 did Yamamoto authorize such a revolutionary move.

Accordingly, the 1st Air Fleet, also known as the Mobile Fleet, was established in April 1941. As was the norm in the IJN, it was commanded by a non-aviator in the form of Vice Admiral Chuichi Nagumo and was comprised of three carrier divisions. The 1st Carrier Division included the large fleet carriers *Akagi* and *Kaga*; the 2nd Carrier Division was assigned fleet carriers *Soryu* and *Hiryu*; and the 3rd Carrier Division had only the old carrier *Hosho* and the light carrier *Ryujo*. Immediately before the war, the new carriers *Shokaku* and *Zuikaku* (the most powerful carriers in the world at the time) were commissioned and formed the 5th Carrier Division. This formation was assigned to the 1st Air Fleet, allowing and the 3rd Carrier Division to be detached for other duties.

The creation of the 1st Air Fleet was revolutionary in concept. It gave the Japanese the means to mass air power at any spot in the Pacific. High-quality aircraft flown by skilled aviators were easily able to overwhelm Allied defenses early in the war. The ability of six fleet carriers to bring 400 aircraft against a single target was

Non-aviator Vice Admiral Chuichi Nagumo commanded the 1st Air Fleet upon its formation in April 1941. He oversaw the attack on Pearl Harbor, and enjoyed further successes in the raid on Darwin and operations against the Royal Navy in the Indian Ocean during the early months of 1942. However, Nagumo's reputation suffered a heavy blow with the defeat at Midway. (NHHC)

OVERLEAF
The locations of principal IJNAF aerial attacks on US Navy ships in 1941–42.

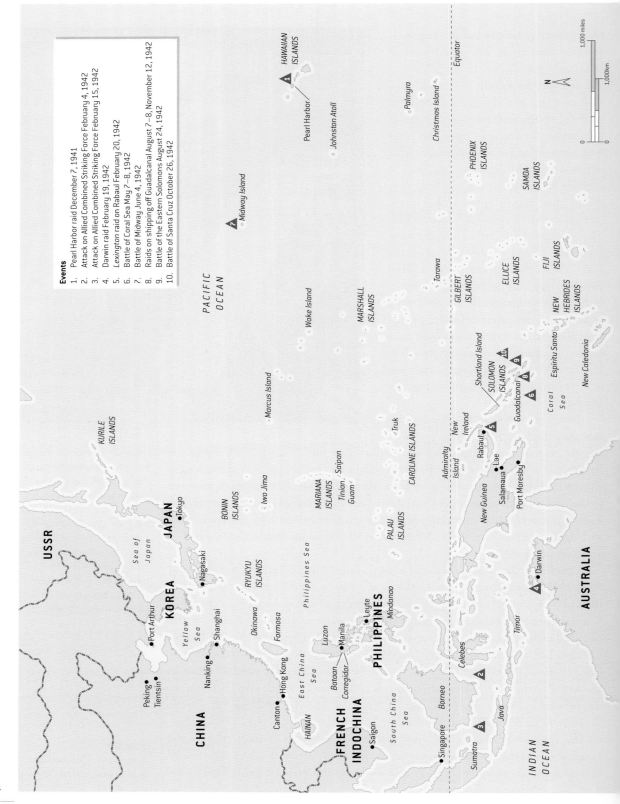

Events

1. Pearl Harbor raid December 7, 1941
2. Attack on Allied Combined Striking Force February 4, 1942
3. Attack on Allied Combined Striking Force February 15, 1942
4. Darwin raid February 19, 1942
5. *Lexington* raid on Rabaul February 20, 1942
6. Battle of Coral Sea May 7–8, 1942
7. Battle of Midway June 4, 1942
8. Raids on shipping off Guadalcanal August 7–8, November 12, 1942
9. Battle of the Eastern Solomons August 24, 1942
10. Battle of Santa Cruz October 26, 1942

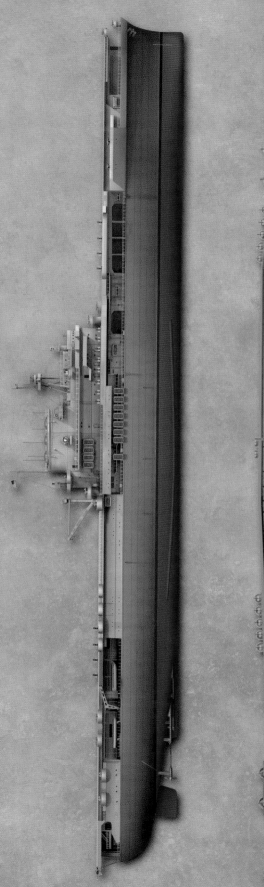

This is the 25,900-ton aircraft carrier USS *Yorktown* (CV-5) as it appeared in the battles of Coral Sea and Midway. Note the heavy antiaircraft armament including eight 5in./38 guns, four 1.1in. quad mounts, and numerous 20mm single guns. Some 824ft 9in. in length and with a beam of 109ft 6in, the five-year-old carrier sank on the morning of June 7, 1942, having been hit by three bombs and torpedoed four times (twice by B5N2s and twice by the IJN submarine *I-168*) the previous day.

irresistible. Ironically, while the IJN was the first navy to concentrate air power into a single formation, it remained wedded to the notion of a decisive battle fought by battleships.

In addition to the carrier force transformation, the 11th Air Fleet was created in January 1941 and assigned three air flotillas with eight subordinate air groups. These were all land-based formations with long-range bombers, fighters, and reconnaissance aircraft. No other navy in the world possessed a force of comparable power. The 11th Air Fleet was an important creation since it had the power and range to cover the invasion of American, British, and Dutch territory in Southeast Asia. This released all six fleet carriers of the 1st Air Fleet for other duties, which eventually became the attack on Pearl Harbor.

The elaborate US Navy pre-war plan to conduct an attack through the Central Pacific toward the Philippines was thwarted during the first hours of the conflict when the US Navy's battle line was devastated in Pearl Harbor. Logistical inadequacies would have made this plan unfeasible anyway (and these were not corrected until late 1943), and following the initial Japanese onslaught throughout the Pacific, the US Navy was reduced to reacting to the enemy's advances. Nowhere was the news good – the Japanese landed large invasion forces in the Philippines and in British Malaya after the IJN had defeated ineffective Allied naval opposition. The British bastion of Singapore fell in mid-February 1942, and the Dutch East Indies surrendered in early March. The last American forces in the Philippines capitulated in early May when no relief operation was mounted to re-supply them. The Americans also lost Guam and Wake Islands and Japanese forces seized Rabaul on January 23.

As the Japanese contemplated their next move, the US Navy was forced to shift to a carrier-centric operations mode following the devastation meted out to its battleships during the Pearl Harbor strike. At the start of the Pacific War, the Pacific Fleet possessed three carriers – *Enterprise*, *Lexington* and USS *Saratoga* (CV-3). *Yorktown* returned to the Pacific in January 1942 and the newly-built *Hornet* arrived in March. The US Navy's other frontline fleet carrier, *Wasp*, was committed in the Atlantic and Mediterranean and would not arrive in the Pacific until June. The final carrier, *Ranger*, was not assessed to be suitable for combat duties in the Pacific.

By early 1942 five carriers were available for operations against the Japanese. Each of these were assigned an escort of two to four light and heavy cruisers and six to eight destroyers. As the Japanese completed their initial phase expansion operations, their attention turned to additional conquests in the South and Central Pacific. The clash between the IJN's maritime strike aircraft and their principal targets, the US Navy's carrier task groups, would not be long in coming.

THE COMBATANTS

IJNAF AVIATORS

The selectivity and intensity of Japanese flight training is well known. Aircrew came from three sources – a small number of Naval Academy graduates, enlisted personnel accepted for flight training, and candidates from civilian life. Some 90 per cent of aviators were enlisted personnel. Basic flight training gave new pilots about 300 hours of experience, after which, from November 1938, those selected to fly attack aircraft undertook a nine-month course of instruction on bombing, observation, and communications. After this the new pilot was sent to his operational squadron.

The problem with the IJNAF's pilot training system was not the quality of the aviators that it produced until 1940, but the quantity of them. Quality was an obsession of the IJN in all fleet components, and this in turn meant that the mass training of pilots was undertaken until the year preceding the outbreak of war in the Pacific. The result was that the IJNAF had a small pool of well-trained aviators entering the war. Of the 3,500 IJNAF pilots in total, an estimated 900 of them had been intensively trained and were rated as outstanding. These were the best in the world at the time, and most were assigned to carrier squadrons, which always had first pick.

The training required to fly a torpedo-bomber was challenging. The pilot had to quickly calculate the target's course, speed, and potential evasive action while simultaneously determining his own action. He had to calculate the release angle for his torpedo, maintain the correct altitude, and drop at the optimum distance from the target. The latter was key since the pilot wanted to get close to the target in order to minimize the effects of target evasion. However, he did not want to get so close

that the torpedo did not have time for its detonator to activate. All of this was done by the pilot using his instinct and naked eye, and often with his aircraft coming under enemy fire.

As they continued their strenuous training, IJNAF torpedo-bomber pilots grew in confidence. In 1932, they registered a hit rate of 60 per cent against moving targets, and this grew to 88.4 per cent the following year. By 1935, the IJNAF came to expect an average hit rate of 70–80 per cent, since pilots often scored a 100 per cent hit rate under ideal conditions and 50 per cent in the worst conditions.

Highly trained B5N2 aircrew pose for a photograph on *Kaga*'s flightdeck the day before their surprise attack on Pearl Harbor. Only a handful of these naval aviators have been identified, namely, first row, fourth from left, PO3c Yuji Akamatsu; second row, third from left, Lt Ichiro Kitajima, fourth from left, Lt Minoru Fukuda, and fifth from left, WO Takayoshi Morinaga; and fourth row, sixth from left, PO2c Takeshi Maeda. Kitajima led 12 B5N2s from *Kaga* in the torpedo attack on Battleship Row. *Kaga*'s level-bombing formation, led by Lt Cdr Takashi Hashiguchi, participated in the sinking of the battleship USS *Arizona* (BB-39).
(Tony Holmes Collection)

Land-based bomber crews also trained hard in torpedo tactics. Released from the war over China, in which they only used bombs against land targets, G3M and G4M crews began to train in the use of the Type 91 torpedo during 1941. This effort was led by the Kanoya Kokutai (Air Group), which was newly equipped with the G4M bomber.

Training for dive-bombing was difficult since inexperienced pilots had great difficulty judging the angle of their approach to the target. This was overcome with more practice, but even more challenging was judging changes in wind direction – these could throw off the pilot's aim unless he made the appropriate corrections.

Early dive-bombing tactics called for pilots to commence their attacks from about 10,000ft, and to maintain the correct dive angle until they were about 3,000ft above the target, at which point the pilot began to aim with the help of a bombsight. The typical bomb release altitude was 1,500ft. To aid training, in 1935 the IJN built a full-size mock-up of a Saratoga-class carrier at a bombing range. Results were good against this target.

The IJNAF had high expectations for its dive-bomber units, based on their success against moving targets during fleet exercises. Dive-bomber pilots were considered an elite, and they trained hard to perfect their craft. In exercises held in 1939, they achieved an accuracy rate of 53.7 per cent. The following year, a 55 per cent accuracy rate was achieved using only the D3A1.

US NAVY CREWMEN

In 1941–42, the crews manning US Navy ships were still volunteers since conscription did not commence until December 1942. Many sailors spent considerable periods of time embarked in the same ship, making for tight-knit crews. Their overall level of training and education during this period was high.

LT CDR TAKASHIGE EGUSA

One of the IJNAF's most outstanding attack pilots, Takashige Egusa was born on September 29, 1909 in Arima-mura village, Ajima County, in Hiroshima Prefecture. The third son of the local village headman, he subsequently attended the IJN's Naval Academy at Etajima, near Hiroshima. After graduation in 1929, he became a naval aviator in 1932. Egusa specialized in dive-bombing from an early stage in his career. From 1934–36 he was assigned to several land-based air groups, before being transferred to the light carrier *Hosho*'s air group in 1937. *Hosho* conducted combat operations off the Chinese coast, striking targets inland, and it was here that Egusa received his first combat experience while flying the D1A Type 94.

In 1939, he was assigned to the air base at Yokosuka as an instructor, and it was during this period that Egusa was recognized as one of the IJNAF's leading dive-bombing experts. Immediately prior to the outbreak of the Pacific War, he was embarked in the carrier *Soryu* as leader of the ship's carrier bomber squadron.

As the leading dive-bomber pilot of his day, Egusa was often given responsibility for leading the D3As from the all carriers in the IJN's task force as it rampaged across the Pacific in the opening months of the war. Indeed, he had led the D3As of the second wave attack on Pearl Harbor on December 7, 1941, personally bombing the battleship USS *Nevada* (BB-36). Despite Egusa's success, the dive-bombers' performance during the raid was generally seen as weak by the IJNAF. However, Egusa's crews subsequently came into their own as potent ship-killers during the February 19, 1942 attack on Darwin and against warships of the Royal Navy in the Indian Ocean in April of that same year. Egusa hit the cruiser *Dorsetshire* and the carrier *Hermes* as the IJN ranged west.

Soryu was part of the Japanese armada that converged on Midway in June 1942, and although Egusa was by then commander of the carrier's air group, he flew no sorties during the pivotal battle and was badly burned when *Soryu* was hit by US Navy SBD Dauntless dive-bombers. After a lengthy recovery, he was assigned to the land-based 521st Kokutai equipped with new Yokosuka P1Y "Frances" twin-engined torpedo-bombers.

On June 15, 1944 off Guam, in the Northern Mariana Islands, Egusa found himself leading a small force of P1Ys against a powerfully defended US Navy Fast Carrier Task Force sent to support the invasion of Saipan. All of the aircraft in the formation, including the P1Y flown by Egusa, were unceremoniously shot down before they reached their targets. None of the aircrew involved survived. By the time of his death, Egusa was among the last aircrew survivors from the men who had attacked Pearl Harbor two-and-a-half years earlier. The ranks of this once elite force had been drastically thinned during the carrier clashes in the Battles of the Coral Sea and Midway and then utterly decimated in the war of attrition that followed in the Solomon Islands.

Acknowledged throughout the IJNAF as its finest dive-bomber pilot, Lt Cdr Takashige Egusa led the D3A1s of the second wave during the attack on Pearl Harbor. (Tony Holmes Collection)

Officers were proficient in technical and operational matters, most having graduated from the Naval Academy located in Annapolis, Maryland. This quickly changed, however, as the fleet expanded. Major commands, like destroyers up through to carriers, were held by Annapolis graduates. For the most part, these officers were not just technically able but were adaptable to changing conditions. One trait which was instilled from the first days at Annapolis was aggressiveness. By law, the commanding officers of carriers had to be qualified aviators, with most being late-career transfers from the surface fleet. This latter point meant that they were not strangers to ship handling.

Enlisted men were also well-educated with at least a high-school degree. These men entered the US Navy for the lure of foreign travel and adventure. During the Great Depression, fewer opportunities existed in civilian life, so qualified men entered the US Navy for the basics – guaranteed accommodation, food, and regular pay. All enlisted men received a 12-week period of basic training, followed by assignment to their first ship, where they were expected to learn a particular skill. Once this had been acquired, and the sailor had demonstrated reliability and leadership, he would be promoted to petty officer. Long-serving personnel could become chief petty officers who possessed exceptional technical skills and leadership qualities. These men were critical to the smooth operation of the ship.

The actual training program aboard ship was largely left up to the discretion of the commanding officer. He decided which areas to stress or not. Basic warfare skills, like antiaircraft gunnery, were a staple on most ships' training schedule. Intensive training was utterly essential to master the art of antiaircraft gunnery. The period before the war was marked by the Great Depression, which reduced opportunities to train. Effective training was expensive, since it consumed ammunition and fuses at prodigious rates. The lack of realistic antiaircraft training was apparent when the US Navy introduced target drones in 1939 that even good crews had difficulty knocking down.

The US Navy underwent a dramatic pre-war and early war expansion that was accompanied by a series of "growing pains". Aside from shortages in modern antiaircraft guns, there were problems training personnel to use them. Many of the new personnel had no training in technical schools so had difficulty in mastering the operation of increasingly complex equipment like the Mk 37 fire control system. Antiaircraft exercise scores dropped between 1939 and 1941 even though targets were only using basic evasive maneuvers. This prompted an intensification of antiaircraft training on many ships. Constant and realistic training directly translated into combat effectiveness.

Going into the Pacific War, many US Navy ships still relied on the 0.50in. water-cooled antiaircraft machine gun as their principal short-range air defense weapon. The gun's modest range and small unexploding round made it unsuitable in this role, and the weapon was replaced by the 20mm Oerlikon gun as soon as production allowed. This view of new recruits being trained on the 0.50in. gun was taken at an unidentified location before the war. (NHHC)

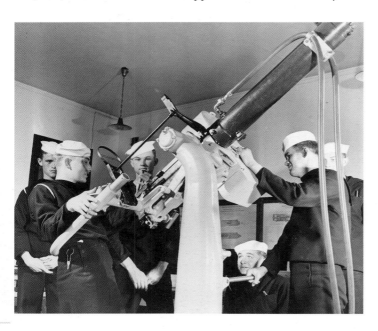

VICE ADMIRAL ELLIOTT BUCKMASTER

Buckmaster was typical of the high caliber of US Navy officers that commanded American carriers early in the war. Born in Brooklyn, New York, on October 19, 1889 and raised in Charlottesville, Virginia, from the age of 12, he enrolled in the US Naval Academy in Annapolis in 1908 and graduated with the Class of 1912. Buckmaster assumed duties as a surface warfare officer and received his first command – of the new destroyer USS *Farragut* (DD-348) – in 1934.

Following this tour, then Cdr Buckmaster applied for flight training at Naval Air Station (NAS) Pensacola, Florida. He graduated in 1936 at the age of 47. It was not unusual for senior officers to enter the aviation community, having either become proponents of naval aviation or because they believed advancement in rank via aviation was quicker. By law, commanding officers of "aviation ships" (mainly carriers) and naval air stations had to be qualified aviators. In 1938 Buckmaster joined the carrier *Lexington* as its executive officer. Following this tour, he was promoted to captain and given command of NAS Ford Island in Hawaii. Buckmaster's performance here gained him command of the carrier *Yorktown* on February 5, 1941.

Under Buckmaster's command, *Yorktown* was perhaps the Pacific Fleet's best carrier in the opening months of the war, its air group performing well at the Battle of the Coral Sea and clearly being the most effective during the Battle of Midway. Buckmaster was concerned about the Japanese air threat, and when *Yorktown* received new 20mm guns he refused to relinquish the old 0.50in. machine guns, as he wanted his ship to be as heavily armed as possible.

Under Japanese air attack at Coral Sea and Midway, Buckmaster handled his ship well, no doubt assisted by his background as a surface officer. At Midway, however, his luck ran out at the hands of *Hiryu*'s skilled aviators on June 4. After *Yorktown* took two torpedoes that knocked out power and created a list of 26–28 degrees, Buckmaster ordered the ship abandoned out of concern for the crew's safety. After the ship did not sink, he and a salvage crew re-boarded the carrier to save it. These attempts seemed ready to pay off when the IJN submarine *I-168* put two more torpedoes into *Yorktown* on the afternoon of June 6 and the carrier sunk shortly thereafter. Buckmaster's career was not ended by what some considered as *Yorktown*'s premature abandonment. Indeed, he was promoted to rear admiral and

named the first Chief of Naval Air Primary Training. Buckmaster subsequently held a series of important jobs in naval aviation training billets until becoming Commander, Western Carolines Operating Area, during the final stages of the Pacific War. Retiring as a vice admiral in 1946, Buckmaster passed away in Coronado, California, on October 10, 1976.

Elliott Buckmaster, pictured as a commander. His lack of aviator wings dates the photograph from before 1936, when he graduated from flight school. (NHHC)

This amazing photograph was taken during the early moments of the Pearl Harbor raid. It shows the B5N2 torpedo-bomber attack in progress against ships moored on both sides of Ford Island. A torpedo has just hit *West Virginia* on the far side of Ford Island, marked by the large plume of water. Other battleships moored nearby are, from left to right, *Nevada*, *Arizona*, *Tennessee* (inboard of *West Virginia*), *Oklahoma* (torpedoed and listing) alongside *Maryland*, and *California*. On the nearest side of Ford Island are the light cruisers *Detroit* and *Raleigh*, the target ship *Utah* and seaplane tender *Tangier*. *Raleigh* and *Utah* have been torpedoed, and *Utah* is listing sharply to port. B5N2s are visible in the right center over Ford Island and over the Navy Yard at right. (NHHC)

COMBAT

PEARL HARBOR ATTACK

The power of the IJNAF's maritime attack aircraft was displayed at the very start of the Pacific War. The devastation caused during the Pearl Harbor attack on December 7, 1941 was an exceptional case since it caught the US Navy's Pacific Fleet unprepared and in harbor. Nevertheless, the results were so overwhelming that the raid gave notice that the IJN's air force had changed the rules of naval warfare.

Since 1939, the IJN had been looking to modify the Type 91 torpedo in order to allow it to attack ships in shallow harbors. This work assumed greater importance in 1941 when the Japanese began serious exploration into the feasibility of an attack on Pearl Harbor. To enter the water at the correct angle, the torpedo had to be controlled in flight. Engineers solved this problem by adding wooden extensions to the fins at the rear of the torpedo so as to reduce pitch and yaw. The wooden fins broke off when the torpedo hit the water and thus did not interfere with the underwater performance of the weapon.

This clever solution, later arrived at by the US Navy as

The main targets along Battleship Row took the most severe pounding. USS *West Virginia* (BB-48) was hit by a probable seven torpedoes, USS *Oklahoma* (BB-37) was hit by a least five, USS *California* (BB-44) took two, and *Nevada* one. All sank or were beached, but only *Oklahoma* failed to return to service. The 16 aircraft sent against the carriers were thrown into confusion when they discovered that their targets were at sea. They instead put single torpedoes into the light cruisers USS *Helena* (CL-50) and USS *Raleigh* (CL-7), neither of which sank, and hit the worthless target ship USS *Utah* (AG-16) with two torpedoes, sinking the former battleship. In return, five of the torpedo-equipped B5N2s were shot down, with a sixth later forced to ditch.

well, was still not enough to facilitate the use of the torpedo in the shallow waters of Pearl Harbor. It was up to the IJN's leading torpedo expert, Lt Cdr Shigeharu Murata, to oversee the effort to develop the correct speeds, drop heights and approaches that would control the torpedo's dive angle so it would not get stuck in the mud at the bottom of the harbor.

The key to the success of the attack was 40 B5N2s armed with torpedoes. Led by Murata himself, 24 were assigned to attack Battleship Row while the remaining 16 targeted the eastern side of Ford Island where the American carriers were usually moored. As a result of their extensive preparations, the Japanese expected 27 hits. The actual results failed to meet this high standard, but were impressive enough. Of the 36 torpedoes launched, the best assessment is that 19 hit.

The main targets along Battleship Row took the most severe pounding. USS *West Virginia* (BB-48) was hit by a probable seven torpedoes, USS *Oklahoma* (BB-37) was hit by a least five, USS *California* (BB-44) took two, and *Nevada* one. All sank or were beached, but only *Oklahoma* failed to return to service. The 16 aircraft sent against the carriers were thrown into confusion when they discovered that their targets were at sea. They instead put single torpedoes into the light cruisers USS *Helena* (CL-50) and USS *Raleigh* (CL-7), neither of which sank, and hit the worthless target ship USS *Utah* (AG-16) with two torpedoes, sinking the former battleship. In return, five of the torpedo-equipped B5N2s were shot down, with a sixth later forced to ditch.

Forty-nine additional B5N2s were employed as level bomber, dropping the special 1,760lb armor-piercing bombs against Battleship Row. They achieved ten hits – better than what they expected. However, of the ten, six failed to explode or were low-order detonations. All that mattered was that one of the two hits on the USS *Arizona* (BB-39) led to a magazine explosion and the battleship's complete destruction.

Surprisingly, the 78 IJNAF dive-bombers committed to the attack accomplished comparatively little. D3A1s from *Akagi*, *Kaga*, *Soryu*, and *Hiryu* were part of the

This is a vertical view of Battleship Row taken from a B5N2. Ships visible from left to right are *Nevada*, *Arizona* with repair ship *Vestal* moored outboard, *Tennessee* with *West Virginia* moored outboard, *Maryland* with *Oklahoma* moored outboard, and the oiler *Neosho* partially visible at the extreme right. A bomb has just hit *Arizona* near the stern, but it has not yet received the bomb that detonated its forward magazines. *West Virginia* and *Oklahoma* are already gushing oil from their multiple torpedo hits and are listing to port. Indeed, the latter ship's port deck edge is already underwater. (NHHC)

43

This panoramic view of Pearl Harbor was taken during the second wave attack. Much can be discerned from this photograph. The large column of smoke in the lower-right center is the burning *Arizona*. The two smoke columns to the left are from the destroyers *Shaw*, *Cassin*, and *Downes*, burning in two dry docks. Note the heavy antiaircraft fire that proved US forces recovered quickly from their initial shock. Most importantly, this photograph reveals why the dive-bombers in the second wave scored so poorly. Not only did they have heavy smoke and antiaircraft fire to contend with, but there was also a low blanket of cloud cover over the harbor area. (NHHC)

second attack wave under the personal command of Lt Cdr Takashige Egusa. Much was expected of these elite airmen, but on December 7 their efforts were blighted by poor marksmanship and weak target selection. Even though they were ordered not to attack battleships since their 551lb bombs could not penetrate their armor, some 30 pilots still went after them. *Nevada* was moving down the channel when the second wave arrived, and 14–18 D3As decided to attack it. The battleship was hit by six bombs and beached. *California* was also hit by a bomb, as was USS *Pennsylvania* (BB-36) in dry dock. Bombs also hit the destroyers USS *Cassin* (DD-372) and USS *Downes* (DD-375) in the same dry dock, destroying them both. Sister-ship USS *Shaw* (DD-373) in another dry dock was hit by three bombs and badly damaged.

These minor successes cost the IJNAF 14 dive-bombers. Japanese crews claimed 49 hits, but the actual number was probably 15. Why did the highly touted dive-bomber pilots achieve a mere 20 per cent hit rate against mostly stationary targets? Among the several reasons were heavy antiaircraft fire by this point and smoke drifting over the harbor from ships struck in the first wave. The biggest reason, however, was a 70–90 per cent low overcast that blanketed the harbor.

DESTRUCTION OF FORCE Z

The attack on two Royal Navy capital ships in the South China Sea on December 10, 1941 demonstrated for the first time the effectiveness of air power against ships at sea. Although not made against ships of the US Navy, it is still illustrative of the tactics and effectiveness of the IJN's land-based air forces. The Royal Navy had assembled Force Z, consisting of the modern battleship HMS *Prince of Wales*, the dated battlecruiser HMS *Repulse* and four supporting destroyers, and sent it to Singapore in an effort to reinforce the British garrisons in the Far East in response to Japanese aggression in the region.

The IJNAF was given the task of neutralizing Force Z, and it planned to do so using 72 G3M and 26 G4M bombers based near Saigon. The G4Ms were from the

Kanoya Kokutai, which was considered the IJNAF's best land-based torpedo bomber group.

After locating Force Z the Japanese prepared to attack, with 59 G3Ms from the Genzan and Mihoro Kokutai dropping ordnance from about 10,000ft. The latter were 550- or 1,100lb bombs without the power to penetrate battleship armor – all the heavy 1,760lb armor-piercing bombs had been allocated to the Pearl Harbor attack force. The remaining 25 G3Ms involved in the attack carried a single Type 91 torpedo, as did the 26 G4M1s of the Kanoya Kokutai.

Since the Japanese bombers had not all taken off together and were duly strung out in a series of scouting lines, the battle developed into a series of attacks. The first, by eight G3Ms, was aimed at *Repulse*. Of the 16 bombs dropped only one hit, inflicting minor damage. The second attack by 17 G3Ms with torpedoes was more successful. Nine went after *Repulse*, but the battlecruiser avoided them all. The eight aircraft that selected *Prince of Wales* as their target scored two hits on the port side aft, buckling the outer propeller shaft. These were critical hits since they caused severe flooding, resulting in a 11.5-degree list that cut the ship's speed to 15 knots and caused power outages. Six more G3Ms attacked *Repulse* with bombs, but all missed.

The third attack featured eight G3Ms with torpedoes, and these were launched at *Repulse* – again, all missed. The 26 G4M1s of the Kanoya Air Group constituted the next wave, and this attack was decisive. Although only six aircraft went after *Prince of Wales*, the battleship was unable to maneuver and four of the torpedoes dropped hit their target. The remaining 20 aircraft targeted the elusive *Repulse*. The IJNAF aircraft conducted a "hammer and anvil" attack that placed the ship's captain in an impossible situation. Unable to evade, the battlecruiser was hit by five torpedoes that caused it to quickly list and sink. A final attack by seven G3Ms with 1,100lb bombs on *Prince of Wales* resulted in one hit that saw the weapon penetrate to the main armored deck and explode, inflicting heavy casualties amongst the crew. Less than an hour after *Repulse* sank, *Prince of Wales* also slipped under the waves.

The price to the IJNAF for destroying the backbone of Allied naval power in the Far East was three aircraft destroyed and 27 damaged. The Royal Navy had clearly underestimated the power and range of the IJN's land-based air force. This was the high-point of Japan's land-based bomber force, since it proved unable to replicate such dramatic results in future attacks against the US Navy.

DUTCH EAST INDIES CAMPAIGN

The Dutch East Indies were defended by a hodge-podge of Allied ships formed into the American-British-Dutch-Australian Combined Striking Force (CSF) on February 1, 1942. Under the command of Dutch Rear Admiral Karel Doorman, the CSF had the near-impossible task of defending Java from Japanese invasion. The

The IJNAF's land-based bombers were tasked with sinking Force Z's *Prince of Wales* and *Repulse*, dispatching 72 G3Ms and 26 G4Ms from an airfield near Saigon. This photograph was taken during the early stages of the attack, which had seen eight G3Ms target *Repulse* – at the bottom of this image – with 16 bombs (both 550- and 1,100lb weapons). Only one hit, inflicting minor damage. (NHHC)

CSF's biggest weakness, among many, was its inability to defend against air attack, and the Japanese exploited this fact several times during the campaign.

On two occasions the CSF faced large-scale Japanese air attacks. The first occurred on February 4 during the Battle of Makassar Strait when four cruisers (including the American heavy cruiser USS *Houston* (CA-30) and the light cruiser USS *Marblehead* CL-12)) and seven destroyers (four American and three Dutch) came under air attack from 36 G4Ms and 24 G3Ms. The CSF was en route to challenge the Japanese invasion force heading for the cities of Makassar and Banjarmasin in the Celebes. None of the bombers carried torpedoes, which were in short supply – only 550- and 132lb bombs were available.

On a brilliant day with unlimited visibility, the Japanese selected the cruisers for attack. The first and second groups of bombers attacked in nine-aircraft sections, the first straddling *Marblehead* but gaining no hits and the second targeting *Houston*, again without success. The third section of seven bombers came after *Marblehead*, and this time scored two hits with 132lb bombs. The 18-year-old cruiser had only 1.5in. of horizontal armor that allowed even the small bombs to penetrate and do serious damage. The first hit forward and started a fire and the second struck the quarterdeck aft, penetrating to the steering compartment, where it jammed the rudder in a hard turn to port. A near miss off the port bow caused flooding.

The next wave selected *Houston* for attack, but all bombs missed. The Dutch cruiser *De Ruyter* was then targeted, although it also avoided being hit. The final attack again saw aircraft go after *Houston*, which was the largest ship in the force. The very last bomb dropped glanced off the heavy cruiser's mainmast and exploded over the main deck between the mainmast and the aft 8in./55 turret. Fragments penetrated the lightly-armored turret, causing the powder bags inside to catch fire. Although the turret crew was killed, damage control efforts contained the subsequent fire.

The first IJNAF air attack against US Navy units at sea had been devastating. *Marblehead* was forced to leave the theater and did not return, although the damaged *Houston* remained in the fight. Without air cover Doorman called off the operation, and the Japanese invasion of Makassar and Banjarmasin went unchallenged. Allied antiaircraft fire proved utterly ineffective, and only adept ship-handling by the cruisers' captains avoided further damage.

The second IJNAF air attack on the CSF occurred on February 15 when a force of five cruisers and ten destroyers (six American) attempted to attack a Japanese invasion force bound for Sumatra. The Allied warships were detected by Japanese search aircraft in the morning and subjected to a day-long assault by B5N1s from the light carrier *Ryujo* and land-based bombers. None of the aircraft had torpedoes, so all attacks were conducted with bombs from high altitude. A total of 30 B5N1 sorties were flown, with 67 land-based

The light cruiser *Marblehead*, a dated Omaha-class ship, photographed at Tjilatjap, Java, after it had been damaged by a Japanese high-level bombing attack in the Java Sea on February 4, 1942. This view shows the effect of the 132lb weapon that struck the cruiser astern. Against the ship's thin 1.5in. horizontal armor, even these small bombs were effective. (NHHC)

bombers also committed to attacks. Although no Allied ships were hit, several sustained minor damage due to near misses – these included two American destroyers. No aircraft were shot down, but Doorman again decided to abort the operation. This episode not only demonstrated the difficulty in hitting maneuvering ships from altitude but also the dominance of IJNAF air power in the Dutch East Indies.

For the remainder of the campaign, Japanese air power picked off isolated Allied naval units. February 15 also saw land-based bombers attack *Houston* while escorting a convoy, the heavy cruiser avoiding damage when 36 aircraft dropped their ordnance from high altitude. Four days later, the 1st Air Fleet entered the campaign when it dispatched 188 aircraft to hit the important Allied staging base at Darwin, in northern Australia. Among the eight ships sunk was the destroyer USS *Peary* (DD-226), which was hit by D3A1 dive-bombers.

Following routing of the CSF by cruisers and destroyers of the IJN during the Battle of the Java Sea on February 27, the remaining Allied ships tried to flee the Dutch East Indies for Australia. Few escaped the Japanese net. Among the US Navy ships falling to IJNAF air power was the seaplane tender USS *Langley* (AV-3), heading for Tjilatjap, on the south coast of Java, from Fremantle, Western Australia, with 32 P-40E Warhawks and 33 pilots on board. On the same day as the Battle of the Java Sea, the former aircraft carrier was attacked south of Java by nine G4M1s from the Takao Kokutai. On this occasion, the accuracy of the horizontal attack was astounding. Against a large target moving at about 13 knots,

As a rule, horizontal bombers had severe difficulties hitting targets during the Pacific War. However, on occasion, they could be deadly. One of these instances was recorded on February 27, 1942 when the seaplane tender *Langley*, fully loaded with P-40Es, was attacked by nine Japanese bombers south of Java. The slow, unprotected ship was hit by five bombs and suffered three near misses, forcing it to be scuttled. (NHHC)

five direct hits and three near misses were recorded that resulted in *Langley*'s abandonment and subsequent scuttling.

On March 1 the destroyer USS *Pope* (DD-225) was attempting to flee from IJN heavy cruisers when a near-miss by attacking Mitsubishi F1M2 Navy Type 0 floatplanes (each armed with two 132lb bombs) and B5N1s (carrying a single 551lb bomb each) from *Ryujo* was enough to cause flooding that eventually forced the ship to be scuttled. That same day the destroyer USS *Edsall* (DD-219) was successfully evading a barrage of 14in. and 8in. shells from two battleships and two heavy cruisers from the 1st Air Fleet when 26 D3A1s from *Kaga*, *Soryu*, and *Hiryu* decided its fate. The aircraft scored several direct hits and near misses that set the plucky destroyer on fire and brought it to a halt. *Edsall* was then sunk by naval gunfire.

INDIAN OCEAN INTERLUDE

The 1st Air Fleet was dispatched into the Indian Ocean in April 1942 to attack British naval bases on the island of Ceylon, and it was during this operation that the ship-killing capabilities of the IJNAF's dive-bombers were at their zenith. Although again not targeting US Navy ships, the exploits of the D3A1 crews are worthy of brief coverage as they are illustrative of how proficient Japanese dive-bombers were by then.

After pummeling British shipping and facilities at Colombo on April 5, IJNAF aircraft spotted the heavy cruisers HMS *Cornwall* and HMS *Dorsetshire* some 170 miles west of the Japanese carriers. Doctrine called for a combined torpedo and dive-bomber attack on a ship as well protected as a heavy cruiser, but the reserve B5N2s were not loaded with torpedoes so the reserve force of 53 D3A1s was dispatched to deal with the British force. Of these, 16 still carried 551lb land attack bombs. Conditions for the attack were perfect, and the strike leader, Lt Cdr Egusa, ordered his aircraft from *Soryu* to attack *Cornwall*, while *Hiryu*'s dive-bombers went after *Dorsetshire*. The 17 D3A1s from *Akagi* split their attacks between the two cruisers.

With the wind behind them, the dive-bombers attacked out of the sun bow-on to the cruisers. Virtually every pilot placed his weapon on the target, or gained a damaging near miss. In 17 minutes, both ships were sunk. *Cornwall* suffered nine hits and six near misses, while *Dorsetshire* recorded ten hits and several near misses.

On April 9 the same thing happened to the light carrier HMS *Hermes* after it was spotted off the east coast of Ceylon. All five Japanese carriers within the 1st Air Fleet launched a total of 85 dive-bombers, and in an attack spanning only 15 minutes, 45 of them attacked *Hermes* and claimed an astounding 37 hits – all confirmed by British accounts. The remaining aircraft sought other targets nearby and accounted for the tanker SS *British Sergeant*, the corvette HMS *Hollyhock*, the Royal Fleet Auxiliary oiler *Athelstone* and the small Norwegian freighter SS *Norviken*.

LEXINGTON'S RABAUL RAID

In February 1942 *Lexington* was ordered to attack Rabaul as part of the US Navy's Task

The heavy cruisers *Cornwall* (left) and *Dorsetshire* (right) maneuver in vain as bombs dropped by 53 D3A1s find their mark on April 5, 1942. Both ships were sunk in record time thanks to perfect conditions for dive-bombing – the cruisers were attacked from dead ahead and down sun, which created a blind spot for the ships' antiaircraft gunners. Literally every bomb dropped either struck the cruisers or scored a telling near miss. (Tony Holmes Collection)

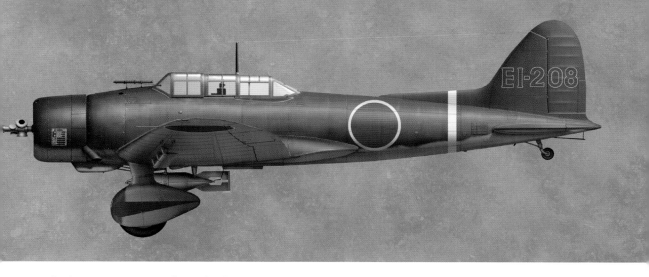

Force (TF) 11. However, on the 20th, the US Navy ships were detected before they could reach strike range and the 4th Kokutai sent out a force of 17 G4M bombers (all armed with two 551lb bombs apiece) from Rabaul's Vunakanau airfield to attack the carrier. The resulting action demonstrated for the first time the shortcomings of such aircraft attacking heavily defended targets without the protection of fighters.

Ships' radar picked up the raiders at a distance of 87 miles and Grumman F4F Wildcats from VF-3 were vectored for an interception. The first group of nine bombers was savaged by the fighters, with only four surviving to drop their bombs – all fell wide. A second group of eight G4Ms faced only a single Wildcat, but its pilot, Lt Edward H. "Butch" O'Hare, knocked down three and damaged two. This left only three bombers to attack *Lexington*, and again all their bombs missed. Of the 17 G4Ms that had attacked, 13 were shot down (only one by antiaircraft fire), two ditched before they could reach Rabaul, and just two damaged aircraft returned to Vunakanau.

BATTLE OF THE CORAL SEA

The world's first carrier clash, the Battle of the Coral Sea was fought between May 4–8, 1942. During this period there were three occasions when IJNAF carrier-based aircraft attacked US Navy ships of TF 17, and these are the focus of the following text.

The first such action occurred on May 7 and is little known. The carriers *Shokaku* and *Zuikaku* formed the *MO* (the IJN designation for the Coral Sea operation) Striking Force and were charged with clearing the Coral Sea of US Navy ships and aircraft so as to allow an invasion convoy to land at Port Moresby in southeastern New Guinea. The IJN knew American carriers were present, but not until May 7 did Rear Admiral Tadaichi Hara, commander of the 5th Carrier Division, receive reconnaissance information that he thought was good enough to launch a strike with.

This dramatic image was a still frame taken from a cine film shot by a sailor on board *Lexington* during the aborted raid on Rabaul by TF 11 on February 20, 1942. FCPO Chuzo Watanabe, flying G4M1 F-348 of the 4th Kokutai, decided to crash into *Lexington*. He missed and flew into the sea just off the carrier's port bow after the bomber had been repeatedly hit by antiaircraft fire from other US Navy ships escorting *Lexington*. Minutes earlier, and just prior to bomb release, the G4M1 had had its port engine and nacelle shot off by Lt Edward H. "Butch" O'Hare, flying an F4F-3 from *Lexington*. (NHHC)

On the morning of the 7th, two B5N2s from *Shokaku* had spotted what was reported as a US Navy surface force that included a carrier. On the strength of this sighting, Hara launched 18 fighters, 26 dive-bombers, and 24 torpedo-bombers. In fact, the initial report had been erroneous – the *Shokaku* aircraft had only spotted an American oiler and its escorting destroyer. Upon learning of this, Hara hastily recalled the fighters and torpedo-bombers. However, *Shokaku*'s air group commander, Lt Cdr Kakuichi Takahashi, unleashed his dive-bombers on the two ships before returning to their carriers – the torpedoes carried by the B5N2s were too valuable to waste.

The dive-bombers made short work of the oiler *Neosho* and the destroyer *Sims*. Four dive-bombers selected the latter for attack and achieved three hits that sank it with heavy loss of life. The remaining aircraft then went after *Neosho*. Seven direct hits and eight near misses were scored against the 7,600-ton oiler, which was left on fire and without power. It did not sink, however, eventually having to be scuttled on May 11. One dive-bomber was shot down by the crew of *Neosho* in return.

The second action involving IJNAF carrier-based aircraft and US Navy ships underway occurred on the afternoon of May 7, and it is even less well known than that morning's one-sided clash. A force of three heavy cruisers (HMAS *Australia*, HMAS *Hobart* and USS *Chicago* (CA-29)), along with two US Navy destroyers, was detached to block any Japanese invasion convoy headed for Port Moresby. This force was within range of Japanese land-based bombers from Rabaul, and at 1400 hrs single groups of G3Ms (from the Genzan Kokutai) and G4Ms (from the 4th Kokutai) began an attack – the latter group of 12 aircraft carried torpedoes.

Unlike in December when Force Z was targeted so successfully, Allied antiaircraft fire was heavy enough to disrupt the attack. The torpedo-bombers were forced to launch their weapons at excessive range and none hit. Furthermore, five G4Ms were shot down, testifying to the effectiveness of the antiaircraft fire. Thirty minutes later, 19 G3Ms with bombs conducted a horizontal attack that was thwarted by skillful maneuvering and concentrated antiaircraft fire. Again, no ships were hit. The weak bombing skills of the Genzan Kokutai G3M crews were matched by their dismal efforts at ship recognition. The aviators involved claimed a California-class battleship and an Augusta-class cruiser sunk, and a Warspite-class battleship and a Canberra-class cruiser damaged.

On May 8 the carriers finally clashed, *Yorktown* launching 39 aircraft and *Lexington* contributing 36 in an attack on the *MO* Striking Force. *Zuikaku* was hidden by clouds and was not damaged. *Shokaku* was struck by three

The US Navy's carrier task force TF 17 was photographed by a Japanese reconnaissance aircraft (almost certainly a B5N2) on May 8, 1942, just prior to it being attacked. The large ship in the center of the task force is *Lexington*. (NHHC)

1,000lb bombs and severely damaged. The Japanese strike against the American carriers caused even more destruction.

Led by Lt Cdr Kakuichi Takahashi at the controls of a D3A1, the IJNAF strike consisted of 18 fighters, 33 dive-bombers and 18 torpedo-bombers. The two US Navy carriers were operating together, with an escort of five heavy cruisers and seven destroyers. When the Japanese aircraft approached TF 17, there were 17 F4Fs aloft on CAP and another 23 SBD Dauntless dive-bombers flying anti-torpedo patrols in the immediate area. On this occasion, the CAP was largely ineffective.

Takahashi ordered his 33 dive-bombers to attack from an upwind position, while the B5N2s descended and commenced their torpedo runs after breaking into two groups – 14 were instructed to attack *Lexington*, while the remaining four went after *Yorktown*. Of the 18 torpedo-bombers sortied, 15 survived fighter interception to launch attacks. When the four aircraft assigned to attack the maneuverable *Yorktown* approached from its port bow, the carrier commenced a starboard turn so as to keep its stern facing the attackers in order to present as small a target as possible. All four launched their weapons, with the final three closing to within 500 yards of their target. The torpedoes missed and two B5N2s were shot down.

In the most important single attack of the battle, the remaining IJNAF torpedo-bombers targeted the unwieldy *Lexington*. The converted battlecruiser was notoriously slow to turn, and to increase their chances of success the Japanese aircraft were divided into two sections in order to attack from either side of the carrier's bow. The first five aircraft – three from *Zuikaku* and two from *Shokaku* – came in from the port bow at 150ft and split into two groups. The carrier managed to turn to port in time to present its stern to the *Zuikaku* aircraft, and their torpedoes all missed. The two *Shokaku* aircraft launched their weapons off the ship's starboard side, and they too missed. This left seven more B5Ns on *Lexington*'s port side.

The carrier made a hard turn to starboard so as to get stern-on to the threat. Upon seeing this, the most northern B5N2s veered off to attack the heavy cruiser USS *Minneapolis* (CA-36), but both their torpedoes missed. The final four aircraft closed to within 700 yards of the carrier before dropping their weapons from 250ft. Although the torpedoes from the first two aircraft ran deep under *Lexington*, at 1120 hrs the final two scored hits on the carrier's port side.

"EI-208" was one of 19 D3A1s from *Shokaku* that attacked *Lexington* on May 8, 1942, the aircraft being photographed at 14,000ft just minutes before it targeted the carrier. What appear to be the wakes of maneuvering ships can be seen behind the dive-bomber. (Tony Holmes Collection)

Several minutes later, Takahashi led the dive-bombers in against TF 17 – the Japanese attack had not been fully coordinated. He detailed his 19 *Shokaku* dive-bombers to attack *Lexington* and the 14 from *Zuikaku* to target *Yorktown*. All 33 were able to deliver their attacks, diving from 14,000ft, unmolested by fighters. The results of the dive-bomber attack were very disappointing for the Japanese. The two carriers were deluged by splashes from ordnance landing close by, but only three bombs hit, and damage was light as a result. The only explanation was the heavy antiaircraft fire put up by the Americans.

Lexington is showered with bombs from 19 D3A1s from *Shokaku*. Fortunately for the ship's crew, only two weapons struck *Lexington*, and these caused light damage. One of the dive-bombers can be seen above the carrier to the right moments after the aircraft had completed its attack. (NHHC)

This somewhat grainy photograph was taken by one of the IJNAF aircraft attacking *Lexington* on May 8, 1942. The carrier is already burning and the number of splashes around the ship indicates this image was taken during the attack by *Shokaku's* dive-bombers. (NHHC)

Against *Lexington*, only two of the *Shokaku* aircraft scored direct hits, the Japanese pilots having held onto their weapons until they were 1,500ft above their target. One bomb hit the forward corner of the flightdeck and the second struck the ship's massive stack, and neither caused significant damage. The last two D3A1s aborted their dives on *Lexington* and went after *Yorktown* instead, but both missed. Two dive-bombers were shot down, one by antiaircraft fire and the other by fighters.

Yorktown was a tougher target, with *Zuikaku's* aircraft having to drop in a crosswind. Only one of the 14 dive-bombers scored a hit. The SAP bomb hit in the center of the flightdeck just forward of the middle aircraft elevator and penetrated four decks before exploding, starting a fire and causing some structural damage. In addition, one near miss amidships on the port side opened several fuel bunkers to the sea that duly created a discernible oil slick.

The two torpedo hits on *Lexington* were ultimately fatal. The first buckled the port aviation fuel tank, causing small cracks to appear that in turn allowed gasoline vapors to spread throughout the ship. At 1247 hrs these fumes were ignited in the forward part of the carrier, resulting in a massive explosion and fires. Two more large explosions sealed the carrier's fate, and its crew were ordered to abandon ship that evening. *Lexington* was later scuttled.

In return for inflicting fatal damage on *Lexington* and striking *Yorktown*, Japanese aircraft losses seemed reasonable – five D3A1s and eight B5N2s had been shot down during the attack. However, overall losses were catastrophic, since seven more aircraft ditched on their way back to the *MO* Striking Force and a further 12 were jettisoned after they had landed aboard *Shokaku* and *Zuikaku* due to the severity of the damage that they had suffered when attacking TF 17. After the recovery on *Zuikaku*, a total of just nine D3A1s and B5N2s remained operational. As a result, Operation *MO* had to be

canceled. Total 5th Carrier Division losses for May 7–8 totaled 69 aircraft of the 109 declared operational before the Battle of the Coral Sea.

The US Navy's after action report acknowledged the skill and bravery of the Japanese aircrew. Most importantly, it recognized that the number of F4Fs available to TF 17 had been woefully inadequate. Furthermore, the CAP had not been deployed sufficiently high enough to stop the D3A1s. The US Navy correctly assessed that antiaircraft fire alone could not stop a determined attack, although it could reduce its effectiveness. Most Japanese aircraft destroyed were not shot down until after they had dropped their weapons, highlighting the fact that the 20mm gun had an effective range of only 1,000 yards. American 5in. guns had achieved some success using barrage fire during the battle. A key conclusion was that the screening cruisers and destroyers were too far from the carriers. The recommendation that they be pulled in to 1,500–2,500 yards was adopted immediately.

BATTLE OF MIDWAY

The carrier battle off Midway Atoll lasted from June 3–6, 1942 and was highlighted by the destruction of four IJN carriers in a series of American air attacks. However, for the purposes of this book, only the two IJNAF air strikes on the US Navy's carrier force on June 4 will be examined.

On the morning of the 4th, US Navy SBD dive-bombers from TF 16 and TF 17 set the carriers *Akagi*, *Kaga*, and *Soryu* afire. All would later sink. This left the 1st Air Fleet with only a single carrier – *Hiryu*. When the smoke cleared from the devastating morning attack, *Hiryu* had just ten A6M2s, eight B5N2s, and 18 D3A1s in operational condition. With these, Rear Admiral Tamon Yamaguchi, commander of the 2nd Carrier Division on board *Hiryu*, decided to launch an immediate strike.

Just before 1100 hrs, a force comprised of six fighters and 18 D3A1s headed west to attack the three American carriers that were less than 100 miles distant. The strike leader, Lt Michio Kobayashi, spotted an American carrier force at 1155 hrs and ordered an attack. This was *Yorktown*, with an inadequate screen of two heavy cruisers and six destroyers. The carrier had just launched 12 Wildcats for CAP, so they were not yet at altitude when Kobayashi's dive-bombers appeared. Nevertheless, in the confusing air battle that followed, the VF-3 CAP was able to destroy or abort 11 of the D3A1s. This left only seven aircraft to attack *Yorktown*.

The experienced Japanese pilots lined up their attack on the carrier's stern, diving from out of the sun. Moments earlier, they had dispersed to attack from several angles to confuse the antiaircraft gunners on *Yorktown*. Of the seven aircraft, three gained direct hits and two more scored damaging near misses. The first two dive-bombers were destroyed by antiaircraft fire, although the remaining five survived. At the end of the attack *Yorktown* was left dead in the water, with thick black smoke issuing from one of the bomb hits.

One of the surviving dive-bombers radioed the results of the attack back to *Hiryu*. Yamaguchi, believing he had knocked one of the three American carriers out of action, prepared a second strike of ten B5N2s (eight fully operational and one damaged but flyable aircraft from *Hiryu* and one from *Akagi*) with six fighter escorts. At 1331 hrs the small force took off and headed west. The strike leader, Lt Joichi Tomonaga, who was also *Hiryu*'s air group commander, spotted what he thought was an undamaged

Lt Michio Kobayashi was the leader of the 24-aircraft-strong strike force dispatched by Rear Admiral Tamon Yamaguchi from *Hiryu* during the late morning of June 4, 1942, shortly after the devastating strike by US Navy carrier aircraft on the 1st Air Fleet. Showing considerable skill and determination during the attack, the pilots of the seven D3A1s that managed to target *Yorktown* achieved three direct hits and two damaging near misses. They paid a heavy price for this success, however, with only five of the 18 that took off from *Hiryu* surviving the mission. Amongst the D3A1s lost to F4Fs or antiaircraft fire was the dive-bomber flown by Kobayashi. (NHHC)

Lt Joichi Tomonaga was *Hiryu's* air group commander during the Battle of Midway. Flying a B5N2, he played an important part in the battle as the leader of the IJNAF strike on Midway Atoll on the morning of June 4, and later as the commander of the second strike on *Yorktown*, which materially contributed to the sinking of the American carrier. Five torpedo-bombers fell to defending F4Fs during the attack on *Yorktown*, including Tomonaga's. (NHHC)

Three B5N2s from *Hiryu* were photographed executing their attack on *Yorktown* in the mid-afternoon of June 4, the aircraft probably being from Tomonaga's group. In the midst of heavy antiaircraft fire, the nearest torpedo-bomber has already dropped its torpedo, while the remaining two are lower and closer to the center of the image. They are flying away from the task force after having also dropped their Type 91s. None of these aircraft achieved any hits. The smoke on the horizon to the right is from a crashed B5N2. (NHHC)

carrier and ordered an immediate attack. In fact this was the patched up *Yorktown*, now making 25 knots.

The CAP interception was thwarted by inadequate numbers of fighters and the efforts of the A6M2 escort. Only one B5N was destroyed before Tomonaga led his force down to their attack altitude of 200ft at a speed of 200 knots. He split his aircraft into two groups to execute the usual "hammer and anvil" attack, with Tomonaga leading the first group. *Yorktown* had turned into the wind to get more fighters on CAP, but this also had the effect of presenting its stern to the approaching Japanese torpedo-bombers. In response, Tomonaga ordered two of his aircraft to attack from the carrier's port side while he and one more B5N2 approached from the starboard quarter.

The first Wildcat off *Yorktown's* deck spotted Tomonaga's torpedo-bomber right after launching, and although the fighter set the B5N2 on fire, Tomonaga kept the aircraft flying long enough to execute a good drop of his torpedo. His sacrifice was not rewarded as the torpedo missed, and he crashed astern of the carrier. Tomonaga's wingman also missed and was shot down by F4Fs as he attempted to exit the area. The two aircraft attacking from the carrier's port side were also unsuccessful, with both being destroyed by fighters or antiaircraft fire.

With the Wildcat pilots predominantly focusing on Tomonaga's four B5N2s and their run at the carrier, the second group of five torpedo-bombers coming in from *Yorktown's* port bow all survived the CAP fighter attacks to reach their launch positions. Four aircraft got their weapons in the water only 600 yards from *Yorktown* and two torpedoes hit on the port side. The effect was devastating, with all nine of the carrier's Babcock & Wilcox boilers being knocked offline and the ship again juddering to a halt with a severe list. The five torpedo-bombers returned to *Hiryu*, together with four surviving fighters.

Following these two attacks, *Hiryu* was left with only four D3A1s and five B5N2s for a third attack on what Yamaguchi erroneously believed was the last remaining American carrier. However, before the planned dusk attack could be launched from *Hiryu*, SBD dive-bombers from *Enterprise* found the carrier and hit it with four bombs, causing fatal damage. Although *Yorktown* was sunk by an IJN submarine on June 7, the Battle of Midway had ended in an obvious victory for the US Navy.

BATTLE OF THE EASTERN SOLOMONS

The Battle of the Eastern Solomons was the first time that US Navy antiaircraft fire played a significant role in a carrier battle. The Pacific Fleet had two carriers present, *Saratoga* and *Enterprise*, but their screens were barely adequate. *Enterprise* was better off since its screen included the modern battleship *North Carolina*. This was the first time a capital ship with its very heavy antiaircraft battery had been integrated into a carrier task force in combat. Also assigned to *Enterprise*'s screen was a heavy cruiser, a light (antiaircraft) cruiser and six destroyers. *Saratoga*'s screen, on the other hand, consisted of only two heavy cruisers and seven destroyers. In accordance with the lessons from the Battle of the Coral Sea, *North Carolina* was positioned 2,500 yards behind *Enterprise*. The cruisers were 2,000 yards from the carrier and the destroyers 1,800 yards away in a circular formation.

The IJN brought fleet carriers *Shokaku* and *Zuikaku* into action during the Battle of the Eastern Solomons. The air group of each consisted of 27 A6M2 fighters, 27 D3A dive-bombers, and 18 B5N2 torpedo-bomber aircraft. The light carrier *Ryujo* was also present, although it was detached with 24 A6M2s and nine B5N2s to neutralize Henderson Field, on Guadalcanal. *Ryujo* was not, as is commonly portrayed, a lure to attract American air attacks.

The carrier clash took place on the afternoon of August 24, with IJNAF reconnaissance aircraft spotting the American warships first. *Shokaku* and *Zuikaku* launched a 73-aircraft striking force at about 1500 hrs, some 54 dive-bombers and 19 fighters taking off in two waves. Vice Admiral Nagumo held his prized torpedo-bombers in reserve in accordance with the new IJN tactical doctrine that stated they should not be committed until the target had been softened up.

The American carriers seemed well-positioned for a successful defense when radar on *Enterprise* detected the first Japanese wave at 101 miles, allowing time for as many as 53 Wildcats to be sent aloft on CAP. However, the fighter interception did not go as planned, since they were held below the 16,000ft altitude of the approaching Japanese strike. Only seven F4Fs were able to attack the D3A1s before they commenced their dives. The Japanese strike commander intended to split his 27 dive-bombers to hit both carriers, but following the battle with the defending Wildcats all surviving "Vals" went after *Enterprise*.

The second group of five B5N2s to attack *Yorktown* on June 4 scored two torpedo hits. Two of the aircraft are visible here, one above the carrier and one astern, after having dropped their torpedoes. On this occasion the heavy antiaircraft fire had failed to protect *Yorktown*. The photograph was taken from the heavy cruiser *Pensacola*, and the destroyer off the carrier's bow is probably *Morris*. (NHHC)

This photograph reveals the bomb damage suffered by *Enterprise* at the Battle of the Eastern Solomons on August 24, 1942. Note the degaussing cables torn from their mountings and the dished-in hull plating at and below the waterline. The carrier is seen in dry dock at the Pearl Harbor Navy Yard on September 10, 1942. Despite the IJNAF having achieved three hits on *Enterprise*, the fact the carrier still remained operational demonstrated the difficulty the IJNAF had in inflicting serious damage on a large ship by using only dive-bombers. (NHHC)

Three dive-bombers struck the carrier with their ordnance, killing 75 and wounding 95, but none of the hits were critical and the ship was able to operate aircraft within an hour after the attack. At least seven of the dive-bombers selected *North Carolina* for attention. No hits were scored, but two near misses caused superficial damage. Of the 27 dive-bombers and ten fighters that made the attack, 17 "Vals" and three Zero-sens were lost. Another dive-bomber and three fighters were also forced to ditch when they exhausted their fuel before they could land back aboard their carriers.

The second Japanese attack wave with 27 dive-bombers and nine fighters seemed poised to finish off *Enterprise*, which, for more than 30 minutes, had been sailing in a circle at reduced speed due to the loss of steering control. With *Enterprise* unable to maneuver, the second striking force passed 57 miles to the south of the ship, before turning to the northwest and heading back to their carriers when no enemy ships could be found. With Nagumo declining to attempt further strikes, the battle was now over.

The American response to the Striking Force attack on *Enterprise* was both uncoordinated and ineffective. Neither of the Japanese fleet carriers were targeted, although carrier aircraft from *Saratoga* found and quickly sank *Ryujo* and damaged the seaplane tender *Chitose*. The battle ended indecisively, although Japanese losses were again heavier due to the destruction of *Ryujo* (along with a destroyer and a transport) and 75 aircraft. *Enterprise* was forced to return to Pearl Harbor for repairs, but only 25 US Navy aircraft were lost.

The US Navy's after action report reflected upon the unsuccessful fighter interception and the fact that the gunners on *Enterprise* and *North Carolina* had no warning of the impending attack until the "Vals" were spotted already in their dives. The Americans counted 15 dive-bombers that made 70-degree attacks on the carrier and did not release their bombs until they were just 1,500ft above their targets. *North Carolina*'s 5in./38 antiaircraft fire was touted as so effective that only a few dive-bombers pressed their attacks home against the battleship. The ship's commanding officer, Capt George H. Fort, credited his 5in./38 crews with five and possibly seven kills. Barrage fire was used to keep a curtain of exploding shells between the ship and the dive-bombers. A 20mm gun with the new Mk 14 gyro sight was credited with downing an attacker at 800 yards. The performance of the battleship was lauded by Pacific Fleet Commander Adm Chester Nimitz, who commented that it was not only a great addition to the carrier's antiaircraft screen but that *North Carolina* drew attackers to itself, thus reducing the weight of attack on the carrier.

BATTLE OF THE SANTA CRUZ ISLANDS

The last carrier battle of 1942 was also the largest, with six such ships being directly involved compared to five at Midway. Santa Cruz was also the only Japanese carrier battle victory of the war, albeit a pyrrhic one since it was the last time the IJN's carrier force was on an equal plane with the US Navy's carrier force.

The battle was driven by Japan's October offensive to seize Henderson Field, on Guadalcanal, with a ground assault. To support the offensive, Adm Yamamoto sent the Combined Fleet to cut off American reinforcements and destroy naval forces in the area. The commander of the American forces in the area, the aggressive Vice Admiral William Halsey, dispatched his only two carriers to meet the IJN warships beyond the range of friendly air support from Guadalcanal. The two Pacific Fleet carriers, *Enterprise* and *Hornet*, were both given strong screens. The flagship of TF 16, *Enterprise* was protected by the recently commissioned battleship USS *South Dakota* (BB-57), a heavy cruiser, an antiaircraft cruiser, and eight destroyers. As the flagship of TF 17, *Hornet* was escorted by two heavy and two antiaircraft cruisers and six destroyers. Together, the two carriers embarked a total of 74 F4F fighters.

Ranged against Halsey's carriers was a larger Japanese force. The Main Body, under Vice Admiral Nagumo's command, included *Shokaku*, *Zuikaku*, and the light carrier *Zuiho*. The two fleet carriers each embarked 21–22 A6M2s, 21–24 D3A1s, and 20–24 B5N2s. *Zuiho* air group consisted of 19 A6M2s and six B5N2s. In addition to Nagumo's carriers, the Japanese readied the 2nd Carrier Division for service in the South Pacific. This formation was comprised of the converted carriers *Junyo* and *Hiyo*. Before the battle, *Hiyo* was forced to withdraw because of an engine room fire, but *Junyo* entered the action with 20 A6M2s, 18 D3A1s, and seven B5N2s. In addition to having more carriers and more aircraft, the Japanese also had the advantage in surface firepower, with a total of four battleships, eight heavy cruisers, two light cruisers, and 24 destroyers committed to the operation.

After a prolonged period of sparring, the two sides closed for action on October 26. The Japanese were organized into three different groups, with *Shokaku*, *Zuikaku*, and *Zuiho* operating together, *Junyo* sailing as part of a separate force to their north, and a number of battleships and cruisers some 70 miles ahead of the Main Body.

The US Navy gained an early advantage when long-range flying boats spotted Nagumo's carriers just before 0300 hrs, the PBY Catalinas even launching an audacious, but unsuccessful, bombing attack on *Zuikaku*. A series of communications problems prevented the Americans from taking advantage of this early break, however. By 0700 hrs, US Navy SBD dive-bombers had sighted all three of Nagumo's carriers, and within an hour *Enterprise* and *Hornet* had both launched a strike that proceeded to the target area in three groups.

This remarkable photograph from the first morning attack on *Hornet* on October 26 shows the high degree of coordination achieved by the IJNAF during the Battle of the Santa Cruz Islands. The aircraft above the carrier is a D3A1 from *Zuikaku*, and it is about to crash into *Hornet's* stack. A B5N2 from *Shokaku* is visible in the background attempting to exit the area after launching its weapon. The photograph was taken from the heavy cruiser *Pensacola*. (NHHC)

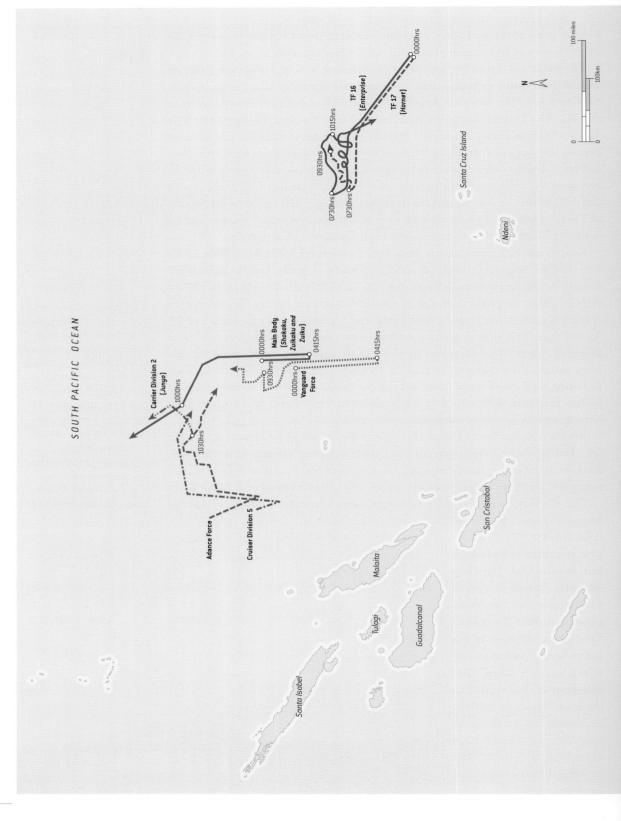

SOUTH PACIFIC OCEAN

Carrier Division 2
(Junyo)

1000hrs

1030hrs

Adance Force

Cruiser Division 5

0000hrs

0930hrs

Main Body
(Shokaku,
Zuikaku and
Zuiku)

0000hrs

Vanguard
Force

0415hrs

0415hrs

TF 16
(Enterprise)

TF 17
(Hornet)

1015hrs

0930hrs

0730hrs

0730hrs

0000hrs

Santa Cruz Island

Ndeni

Santa Isabel

Malaita

Tulagi

Guadalcanal

San Cristobal

N

0   100km
0   100 miles

The Japanese response was much better organized. A *Shokaku* B5N2 made contact with the American carriers at 0612 hrs and Nagumo received the report from this aircraft just before 0700 hrs, the IJNAF strike started to launch just ten minutes later, the three carriers of the Main Body putting up a total of 21 A6M2s, 21 D3A1s, and 22 B5N2, of which only 20 carried torpedoes – the other two were designated as tracker aircraft. The Striking Force was headed by Lt Cdr Shigeharu Murata, the IJN's most acclaimed torpedo-bomber pilot and leader of the B5N2s during their attack on Battleship Row on December 7, 1941.

After the launch of the first wave, two SBD dive-bombers conducted an unopposed attack on *Zuiho*. A single bomb hit started a fire aft and knocked the arresting gear out of action. Unable to recover aircraft, the carrier was forced to withdraw. By 0900 hrs a second wave had taken off from *Shokaku* and *Zuikaku* and was headed towards the American carriers. This Striking Force was split into two groups, with the first consisting of five A6M2s and 20 D3A1s from *Shokaku* and the second consisting of 17 B5N2s (one of which was designated as a tracker aircraft and thus carrying no torpedo) and four A6M2s from *Zuikaku*. These two waves constituted the largest Japanese strike of the war to date directed at a US Navy carrier force.

Murata spotted *Hornet* and TF 17 at 0853 hrs – *Enterprise* was hidden by cloud cover at the time. The sailors manning the American ships knew the Japanese were coming since radar on the cruiser USS *Northampton* (CA-26) had detected the aircraft at 0841 hrs some 70 miles away. Unfortunately for TF 16, this critical information never reached the senior fighter direction officer on board *Enterprise*. Before the attack, *Hornet* had a total of 15 fighters on CAP, but they were not well positioned. Murata immediately ordered the 21 dive-bombers from *Zuikaku*, under the leadership of Lt Sadamu Takahashi, to attack. Eight Wildcats managed to destroy three dive-bombers and severely damage three more in a single high-speed head-on attack. At 0910 hrs, seven "Vals" pushed over into their dives from astern *Hornet*. Of the seven aircraft that attacked, three succeeded in hitting the carrier.

The next to attack were Murata's torpedo-bombers, which he had split into two groups to conduct a "hammer and anvil" attack. Murata led 11 B5N2s to the south and then went into a dive to gain speed. The remaining nine "Kates" headed for the carrier from the north. Seeing this set-up, *Hornet*'s commanding officer, Capt Charles P. Mason, ordered a change of course to the northeast to spoil the "hammer and anvil" attack. This forced Murata to lead his group into a difficult stern attack. Murata and his two wingmen were the first to attack from *Hornet*'s starboard quarter. Despite the unfavorable launch angle, two of the three torpedoes hit the carrier. Two aircraft were shot down, including Murata's. The next section of three aircraft succeeded in launching their torpedoes, but all missed to starboard. The final five "Kates" faced a tactically disadvantageous situation approaching the carrier from astern, and the three pilots that targeted *Hornet* all missed. Two went after the heavy cruiser USS *Pensacola* (CA-24) and also missed.

This attack by Murata's B5N2s was the most important of the entire battle, and it went a long way to deciding who would be the victor. The two torpedoes struck amidships, with one causing much destruction in the engineering spaces. They would prove to be fatal hits. Each time a torpedo (either dropped from an aircraft or fired by a submarine) struck a US Navy carrier during the battles of 1942, the result was the loss of the ship.

OPPOSITE

The Battle of the Santa Cruz Islands on October 26, 1942, from 0000–1200 hrs.

OVERLEAF

The B5N2s of Lt Cdr Shigeharu Murata and his two wingmen approach *Hornet* from the ship's starboard rear quarter on October 26, 1942 during the Battle of the Santa Cruz Islands. In an action lasting just 30 minutes, both D3A1 "Val" dive-bombers and B5N2 "Kate" torpedo-bombers successfully targeted the carrier. Despite being engaged by highly accurate antiaircraft fire, all three "Kate" pilots succeeded in dropping their Type 91 torpedoes, two of which hit *Hornet* and led directly to its loss. Murata did not survive the attack.

Jim Laurier

As Murata's torpedo-bombers were attacking, the second group of "Vals" from *Zuikaku* began their dives. Only five of the seven survived fighter attacks, and of these, four selected the carrier, but all missed. The last aircraft crashed into *Hornet's* island. The final group of D3A1s conducted their attack immediately after the second. Only three survived two different fighter interceptions to dive on *Hornet*, and again all missed.

Next up were the nine torpedo-bombers attacking from the north. These had no fighter escort and were roughly handled by the Wildcats. Three were shot down and one was destroyed attempting to crash into the light cruiser USS *Juneau* (CL-52). The remaining five flew through the defensive screen, with one being shot down in the process by the destroyer USS *Morris* (DD-417). The last four pressed on to launch their weapons within 300–800 yards of *Hornet*, and all missed.

Within minutes of the final torpedo attack, one dive-bomber came in and dropped its weapon 50 yards off the carrier's bow. It then returned to crash onto *Hornet* on its forward port side. Moments later, one of the B5N2s from the second attack group, having jettisoned its torpedo, also attempted to crash onto *Hornet*. The attack failed when the aircraft hit the water forward of the ship.

In a span of less than 30 minutes, the IJNAF had conducted the best coordinated and most effective attack on an American carrier during the entire war. *Hornet* was hit by two torpedoes, three bombs, and two aircraft. With fires raging, the carrier was also left dead in the water as a result of the torpedo hit. This success had come at an extremely high price. Of the 12 fighters, five were lost, of the 21 dive-bombers, 17

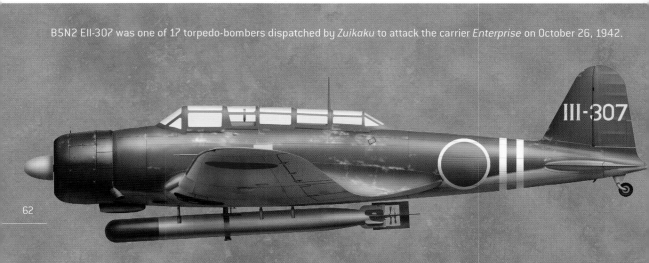

B5N2 EII-307 was one of 17 torpedo-bombers dispatched by *Zuikaku* to attack the carrier *Enterprise* on October 26, 1942.

were lost, and of the 20 torpedo-bombers, 16 were lost.

The second IJNAF attack wave had the opportunity to turn the battle into a decisive Japanese victory. Nagumo was aware of the location of *Enterprise*, and the second wave was directed to this lucrative target. Since the Striking Force was launched in two different groups, there was no possibility of mounting a coordinated attack.

Having made an unsuccessful torpedo attack on *Enterprise*, two B5N2s from *Zuikaku* leave the combat area during the Battle of the Santa Cruz Islands by flying between their target and the battleship *South Dakota*, the bow of which is visible to the left in this photograph taken from the carrier's island. Nine of the 16 torpedo-armed aircraft that had taken off from *Zuikaku* were downed in the attack. (NHHC)

The first group consisted of 19 dive-bombers from *Shokaku* escorted by only four fighters. The approaching formation was detected on radar, but again the 21 Wildcats on CAP were not well positioned to intercept the raid. At 1008 hrs Lt Cdr Mamoru Seki ordered his dive-bombers to attack. Caught at lower altitudes, only two F4Fs managed an interception of Seki's aircraft before they commenced their dives – just one D3A1 was shot down as a result.

Seki set up his attack well, splitting his surviving bombers into three groups to attack *Enterprise* from out of the sun. The groups attacked sequentially, giving the American gunners the chance to engage each dive-bomber as it attacked. *Enterprise's* 5in./38 battery opened fire, as did the identical weapons on board *South Dakota*, which was steaming immediately astern of the carrier. Indeed, the battleship's antiaircraft barrage fire proved to be particularly deadly.

Seki's group of seven aircraft attacked first, although the heavy antiaircraft fire disrupted the pilots' aim and none scored a hit. Seki and three other D3As were shot down. The next group of seven aircraft attacked *Enterprise* from astern only two minutes later. The lead aircraft gained the first hit at 1017 hrs when its bomb struck some 20ft from the bow. The weapon penetrated the flightdeck and forecastle and exploded in the air off the port bow, thus causing little damage. A second hit one minute later just aft of the forward elevator and started a fire among the Dauntless dive-bombers chained down in the hangar deck before penetrating to the second deck, where it exploded and caused severe personnel casualties. At 1020 hrs, a damaging near miss was gained on the ship's starboard quarter.

The 12 dive-bombers of the second and third groups suffered heavily. Six aircraft were shot down, including three by antiaircraft fire. Of the 19 "Vals" that attacked, ten were lost – seven fell to antiaircraft fire and three to fighters.

The dive-bombers failed to cause significant damage to *Enterprise*. Responsibility for finishing the American carrier off fell to Lt Shigeichiro Imajuku, leader of the *Zuikaku* torpedo-bomber squadron. Again, the American CAP was not well handled, and the "Kates" reached their attack positions largely unmolested. Imajuku divided his force into two eight-aircraft sections to employ a "hammer and anvil" attack from either side of the bow. The group led by Imajuku was the first to attack, and although fighters accounted for him, his wingman managed to launch his weapon at *Enterprise's* starboard beam but missed. The next three aircraft also succeeded in launching their torpedoes, and a sharp turn to starboard by the carrier resulted in all three missing.

The next two aircraft were unable to get into a good attack position against *Enterprise*, so they went after *South Dakota* instead. The first launched its torpedo, which missed, and the second was shot down as the "Kate" flew over the battleship's stern after it had released its weapon, which also missed. The final B5N2 of Imajuku's group approached *Enterprise* from dead ahead, and its torpedo missed the carrier by just 300ft on the starboard side. The aircraft was then shot down by the 1.1in. quad mount in the bow of the ship.

To escape serious damage, *Enterprise* had to avoid being hit by the second section of eight B5N2s. As this group began its descent through a bank of clouds, two Wildcats attacked and destroyed one aircraft and made another abort. After the remaining "Kates" emerged from the clouds, they were astern of *Enterprise*. As the torpedo-bombers moved through the carrier's screen, one damaged B5N2 deliberately crashed into the destroyer USS *Smith* (DD-378) and caused heavy loss of life amongst its crew.

As the final five attempted to get into an attack position off *Enterprise*'s port bow, the ship's commanding officer, Capt. Osborne B. Hardison, tried to keep his stern to the attackers. One B5N2 launched its torpedo from dead astern, but it missed and the aircraft was shot down by antiaircraft fire. The last four launched their torpedoes from the carrier's port quarter, but these also missed. Of the 16 B5N2s, nine were able to launch their weapons. Excellent ship handling created poor attack angles that resulted in all torpedoes missing and *Enterprise* avoiding the fate of *Hornet*.

Although the attacks by *Shokaku* and *Zuikaku* were the most important of the battle, others followed. *Junyo* maneuvered into position to launch a strike (consisting of 17 dive-bombers escorted by 12 fighters) from some 320 miles away.

Once again, the American fighters failed to intercept the incoming raid. At 1121 hrs, the first of the dive-bombers appeared out of the clouds and dove on *Enterprise*. The same cloud cover that had protected the dive-bombers from interception now also prevented them from obtaining a good attack position. They targeted *Enterprise* from astern, but did so at a shallow 45-degree angle that increased their vulnerability to antiaircraft fire. Only eight of the dive-bombers dove on *Enterprise*. The first three were all shot down by antiaircraft fire and their bombs missed their target. The fourth aircraft placed its bomb less than ten feet off the port bow, which caused minor flooding and jammed the forward elevator. The remainder of the aircraft missed, but none were shot down by antiaircraft fire.

The other nine *Junyo* "Vals" were unable to keep *Enterprise* in sight through the low clouds, with four selecting to attack *South Dakota* instead. The first three missed, but the last aircraft placed its bomb on top of the forward 16in. gun turret. The latter's heavy armor prevented any real damage being inflicted on it, although several personnel were wounded by shrapnel. The last five *Junyo* dive-bombers attacked the light cruiser *Juneau*, which was part of the screen off *Enterprise*'s port bow. The first three dive-bombers missed, but the fourth gained a damaging near miss and the last to attack hit the cruiser's stern. The SAP bomb penetrated all the way through the ship and exploded underneath the hull. The damage was moderate, with some flooding and a temporary rudder jam. Of the 17 dive-bombers involved, three were shot down by antiaircraft fire and five fell to fighters.

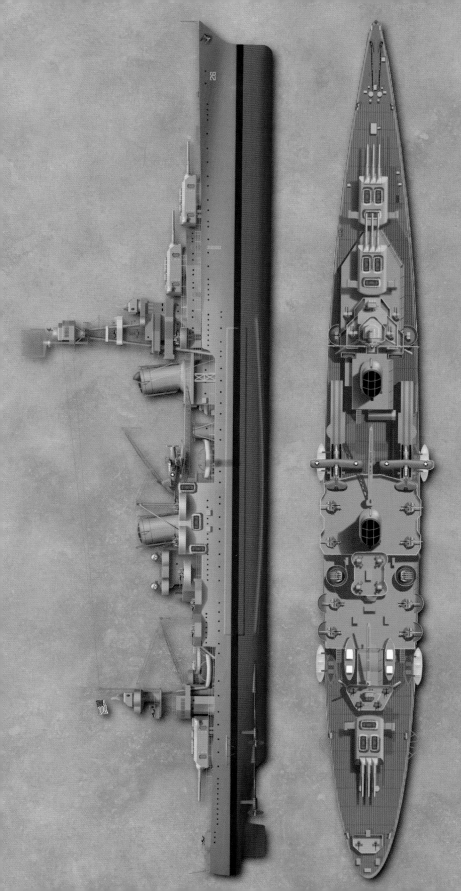

The six heavy cruisers of the Northampton-class were a mainstay of the US Navy's carrier escort force in 1942. This is the lead ship of the class, USS *Northampton* (CA-26), as it appeared in the Battle of Midway. The heavy cruiser's antiaircraft weaponry then consisted of eight 5in./25 guns and two 1.1in. quad mounts grouped centrally amidships either side of the rear stack. *Northampton* attempted to tow the powerless *Hornet* to safety during the Battle of the Santa Cruz Islands on October 26, 1942. The 9,200-ton *Northampton* was torpedoed during the Battle of Tassafaronga on November 30, 1942 and sank the following day.

This initial round of attacks had gone well for the Japanese. Albeit at a very high cost, *Hornet* was crippled and *Enterprise* damaged, but it was still in action. The IJN had erroneously assessed that as many as three US Navy carriers were present, and it sought to finish off the other two thought to still pose a threat. Two Japanese carriers, *Zuikaku* and *Junyo*, remained operational, and these now prepared follow-on strikes against *Enterprise*. What followed was a series of small strikes with whatever aircraft the Japanese could muster. Fortunately for the Americans, the Japanese thought that the two remaining US Navy carriers were operating to the north and northwest of the crippled and stationary *Hornet*. *Enterprise*'s actual position was south of *Hornet*, which meant it was spared further attacks.

Junyo's second strike of the day was launched at 1313 hrs and was comprised of eight A6M2s and seven B5N2s (only six of which carried torpedoes). At the same time, *Zuikaku* launched its third strike of five A6M2s, two D3A1s, and seven B5N2s (six of which carried 1,760lb bombs and one was an unarmed tracker aircraft). These two strikes searched fruitlessly for *Enterprise* until turning south and spotting *Hornet*, which was now under tow by the heavy cruiser *Northampton*. The six torpedo-bombers from *Junyo* were the first to attack. There was no CAP and the crippled carrier was stationary after *Northampton* had cast off the tow line. Nevertheless, only one of the six aircraft scored a hit. Antiaircraft fire downed both the skillful pilot who placed the Type 91 torpedo amidships and a second aircraft. Next to attack were the two dive-bombers from *Zuikaku* – neither was successful.

At this point, *Hornet*'s crew was ordered to abandon ship. As this was proceeding, the six *Zuikaku* B5N2s with their large bombs began their attack run from 8,000ft off the carrier's port quarter. Against a stationary target, the results were disappointing. One bomb hit aft, causing little damage, and the other five missed.

The hard-driving *Junyo* launched a final strike of six A6M2s and four D3A1s at 1535 hrs. These attacked *Hornet* at 1650 hrs, with one of the "Vals" hitting the forward flightdeck with a single bomb that duly penetrated to the hangar deck, causing a fire. After the final air attack, American destroyers were ordered to scuttle the carrier. Despite another 14 torpedo hits (ten from American destroyers and four from Japanese destroyers), the carrier did not go down until the following morning. The final carrier battle of 1942 was over.

This iconic photograph shows torpedo-laden G4Ms from the 4th Kokutai flying at extremely low altitude through antiaircraft fire to attack US Navy transports between Guadalcanal and Tulagi on the morning of August 8, 1942. The image was taken from an American ship, and it clearly shows the potential vulnerability of the bombers to even close-range weapons like the 20mm gun, which were already prevalent at the time. Note the heavy barrage of 5./38 shells in the background. (NHHC)

IJNAF LAND-BASED BOMBERS AT GUADALCANAL

While the carriers dueled only twice during the Guadalcanal campaign, Japanese land-based bombers from Rabaul were constantly looking for an opportunity to attack US Navy warships. Their primary targets were American carriers, but these were usually kept out of range. US Navy ships supporting operations on Guadalcanal were within range, however, and the IJNAF committed its land-based bombers to attacking large convoys off the embattled island on three separate occasions.

This first happened on August 7 during the initial landings by the US Marine Corps on Guadalcanal. In response to reports that the invasion was underway, the Japanese mustered all the aircraft they could from Rabaul and launched an immediate attack. The force consisted of 18 A6Ms and 27 G4Ms (from the 4th Kokutai) armed with bombs. In addition, nine D3A1s were also committed to the attack, even though they did not have the range to return to Rabaul. The IJNAF attack force arrived over Guadalcanal at 1315 hrs. The ships offshore were covered by clouds, but the bombers dropped anyway and scored no hits. The D3A1s arrived at about 1500 hrs and hit a destroyer with a bomb. The attackers were intercepted by carrier-based F4Fs as they withdrew and five G4Ms were shot down and four forced to ditch on the way to Rabaul. All of the D3A1s were lost.

The next day, the Japanese planned another attack. This time, the G4Ms (again from the 4th Kokutai) were loaded with torpedoes, 27 of them taking off from Rabaul escorted by 15 fighters. Unable to find the American carriers, the 23 remaining bombers headed for Guadalcanal to attack the invasion fleet offshore. Of these, three were destroyed by Wildcats before reaching an attack position. The rest of the force came in at very low altitude to drop torpedoes against the transports. The vulnerable G4Ms were savaged by American antiaircraft fire – at such close range, even 20mm guns were deadly. Of the 20 bombers that attacked, only five survived to return to Rabaul. In return, the destroyer USS *Jarvis* (DD-393) was hit by a torpedo and one of the doomed G4Ms crashed into the transport USS *George F. Elliott* (AP-13), causing a large fire that eventually resulted in the ship being scuttled.

On the morning of the 9th, 16 torpedo-armed G4Ms from the newly arrived Misawa Kokutai took off from Vunakanau and went searching for the US carriers and

The largely intact wreckage of one of the 18 G4Ms from the 4th Kokutai that were downed during the disastrous August 8 torpedo attack. This photograph was taken from the destroyer USS *Ellet* (DD-398). (NHHC)

their task force. The only warship they found was the badly damaged *Jarvis*, trying to make it to Pearl Harbor for repairs. Mistaking the destroyer for a cruiser, the G4M crews sank it with two torpedoes, but not before the crew of the *Jarvis* had downed two bombers and damaged a third so badly it crash-landed on Buka.

On August 30, 18 G4Ms (nine from the Kisarazu Kokutai and nine from the Misawa Kokutai) and 13 A6Ms targeted shipping off Guadalcanal. The high-speed troop transport USS *Colhoun* (APD-2) was the subject of the attack. Although the converted destroyer should have been a difficult target to hit with horizontal bombing, Japanese accuracy was impressive on this occasion. Dropping bombs from 15,000ft, crews achieved four direct hits and several near misses, sinking the veteran warship in minutes.

In a repeat of the ill-fated August 8 attack, the Japanese spotted a large American reinforcement convoy off Guadalcanal on November 12. Sixteen G4Ms from the 703rd, 705th, and 707th Kokutai headed down from Rabaul with a heavy escort of 30 fighters. The bombers pressed on through an ineffective American fighter interception to attack the convoy with torpedoes at very low level. The transports were heavily escorted by cruisers and destroyers, and in an eight-minute attack, the Japanese crews bravely pressed home their attacks but were mauled by antiaircraft fire. The attempt by the bombers to target the convoy in a "hammer and anvil" attack was frustrated by adept American maneuvering. Eleven of the bombers were destroyed and the only damage inflicted on an enemy ship came when one of the doomed G4Ms crashed onto the stern of the heavy cruiser USS *San Francisco* (CA-38). Damage was light and it remained in action.

STATISTICS AND ANALYSIS

As powerful as the IJNAF was at the start of the conflict, it also possessed a significant weakness. As combat losses increased throughout 1942, this attrition fully exposed the brittle nature of Japanese naval air power. The IJNAF had been built for fighting a short and decisive war. When the planned short war became a grinding battle of attrition, the Japanese were unable to cope. Even before the conflict in the Pacific had commenced, there were shortages in aircraft, munitions, and fuel.

Another problem area that also existed pre-war was aircrew training. During the IJN's rapid expansion in size in the late 1930s, the IJNAF had struggled to keep pace due to an inadequate training organization, modest facilities, and a paucity of aircraft. By the IJNAF's own standards, half of its aviators were not fully trained at the start of the Pacific War. This had less of an impact on the carrier force since it received the best-trained aviators, but the operational readiness of land-based bomber units was immediately hampered by inadequately trained aviators and aircraft shortages.

The basic characteristics of Japanese aircraft also contributed to the number of losses (both in terms of men and materiel) during 1942. Built for long-range offensive action, the aircraft were lightly constructed in order to keep their weight down so that they could then satisfy the IJNAF's extraordinary range requirements. This meant that Mitsubishi, Nakajima, and Aichi delivered aircraft that lacked armored protection for their crews and self-sealing fuel tanks. Unable to take battle damage, "Vals", "Kates", "Nells", and "Bettys" suffered heavy losses when attacking well-defended targets, which US Navy task forces clearly were. Aircrew losses where correspondingly heavy, and were exacerbated by the fact that the Japanese were operating over enemy territory.

In the first carrier-versus-carrier battle at Coral Sea, the IJNAF showed an ability to strike hard against US Navy surface ships. The second-string aviators of the new 5th Carrier Division were skillful enough to hit both American carriers present. *Lexington* was struck by two torpedoes and two bombs, leaving it badly damaged. Fuel explosions later in the day destroyed the ship, which was the first US Navy carrier sunk during the war. *Yorktown* suffered moderate damage from a single well-placed bomb, although it was repaired in time for the next carrier clash. In the first occasion during the war when IJNAF carrier-based attack aircraft encountered robust air defenses, they suffered heavily. The Japanese lost a total of some 69 carrier aircraft, mostly "Kates" and "Vals".

Midway was unique among the carrier battles of the Pacific War. It was the only time that one side opened the battle with an ambush of the other's carrier force. Because of its superior intelligence, this opportunity went to the US Navy. The opening blow took out three of the 1st Air Fleet's four carriers before their air groups had a chance to engage the American fleet. All the ships' aircraft were lost, but this in turn kept aircrew losses relatively low.

The final carrier, *Hiryu*, gave a fine account of itself, and provided a glimpse into what the outcome of the battle would have been had the remaining three carrier air groups been able to attack. Despite having only 18 "Vals" and ten "Kates", *Hiryu* was able to launch two crippling strikes on *Yorktown* that left the latter badly damaged and created the conditions for its eventual loss. Aircraft attrition had been heavy, but the accuracy of the two strikes were astounding. Of the seven "Vals" that survived the US Navy CAP, three scored hits. Eight "Kates" launched torpedoes at *Yorktown* and two of the weapons hit, sealing the carrier's fate. These two attacks had shattered *Hiryu*'s air group, and it was left with only a handful of airworthy strike aircraft when the carrier was attacked by SBDs on the afternoon of June 4.

Midway was not the end of the IJN's carrier force as many post-war accounts state. Total aircrew losses were limited to 110 personnel, mostly from the *Hiryu* air group. There were certainly enough highly-skilled aviators rescued from *Akagi*, *Kaga*, and *Soryu* to reform the air groups of the only two remaining fleet carriers, *Shokaku* and *Zuikaku*, and to give the light carriers *Junyo*, *Hiyo*, *Ryujo*, and *Zuiho*, all of which fought in the Guadalcanal campaign, more than a token number of experienced aviators.

After the Midway debacle, the IJN changed its organization to put the carrier in a more prominent position. The composition and tactics of Japanese carrier air groups were also modified. The numbers of fighter aircraft in air groups were increased. The Japanese also assessed that torpedo-bombers were more vulnerable than dive-bombers, so the number of dive-bombers was increased at the expense of torpedo-bombers. The vulnerability of torpedo-bombers drove the Japanese to plan to use only dive-bombers in the first attack wave of the next carrier battle. Morale of the Japanese attack aircraft aircrews remained high, and they were confident they had the equipment and training to deal hard blows to the American carriers when the next clash occurred.

The next clash at the Battle of the Eastern Solomons was the most tentative of the four 1942 carrier battles. It ended indecisively, but did account for the light carrier *Ryujo* and 61 more Japanese aircrew.

The Battle of the Santa Cruz Islands was the most illustrative carrier clash of 1942 since it confirmed that the US Navy had made significant advances in fleet air defense, and that these defenses had developed to the point where they were able to inflict

Yorktown dead in the water and listing heavily, shortly after being hit by two Type 91 aerial torpedoes during the afternoon of June 4, 1942. The section of catwalk jutting above the flightdeck, port side amidships, is directly above the location where the torpedoes struck. (NHHC)

A D3A1 burns fiercely after being hit directly over *Enterprise* on August 24, 1942 during the Battle of the Eastern Solomons. Note the antiaircraft shell bursts that have seemingly followed the path of the dive-bomber. Only eight of the 27 D3A1s that attacked the *Enterprise* task force survived to return to their carriers. (NHHC)

crippling attrition on the IJNAF's now obsolescent "Vals" and "Kates". Of the 203 aircraft available to the Japanese at the start of the battle, 99 were lost. Predictably, strike aircraft suffered the highest attrition, with 41 of 63 dive-bombers and 30 of 57 B5N2s being lost. For the first time in 1942 the method of destruction was evenly split between CAP (26) and antiaircraft fire (25). The balance of losses was from operational causes or ditching of damaged aircraft, and one was destroyed aboard the bombed *Shokaku*.

IJNAF carrier aircrew losses were crippling. In total, 145 aircrew (68 pilots and 77 observers), including 23 section, squadron, or air group leaders, were killed. Santa Cruz was the only Japanese victory in any carrier battle during the war, but the extremely heavy aircraft and aircrew losses meant that the IJN was unable to follow up its success. Of the five carriers present at the start of the battle, only *Junyo* and the troublesome *Hiyo* were left in the South Pacific for the next decisive month of the Guadalcanal campaign.

Concurrent with the efforts of its carrier force, the IJNAF's land-based air force fought its own war for the control of the airspace over Guadalcanal and the waters around the island. The great majority of the sorties flown by bombers from Rabaul were devoted to attacking the airfield on Guadalcanal, but on occasion they were directed to attack maritime targets. The IJNAF attempted on several occasions to find and attack the US Navy carriers operating near Guadalcanal but they were never successful in this regard.

Large convoys off Lunga Point were considered lucrative targets, and the IJNAF's "Betty" land-based bombers conducted three large-scale attacks against them. Two of these strikes were made with torpedoes, and thus required the G4Ms to attack at low altitude to penetrate the fighter screen and launch their weapons at the transport ships. This meant that even the short-ranged 20mm guns on the American escorts and transports were now deadly.

Each of the three attacks ended in disaster for the IJNAF, with 38 of 66 attacking G4Ms being lost in return for a transport and a destroyer sunk and a transport, a destroyer, and a heavy cruiser damaged. These losses showed how vulnerable land-based bombers were while conducting torpedo attacks during daylight against well-defended targets. Indeed, the attrition was so high in terms of aircraft lost that they were among the last daylight torpedo attacks undertaken by Japanese land-based medium bombers in World War II.

The US Navy demonstrated a great ability to apply new lessons to the problem of fleet air defense throughout 1942. Fighters were always seen as the preferred method of protecting the fleet, but even though the proportion of Wildcats in carrier air groups went up during 1942, the continuing problems with their direction by carrier-based controllers meant that the CAP was very much an imperfect shield.

As the US Navy struggled to perfect fighter defense of the fleet, it also installed more and better antiaircraft guns on frontline ships. The 20mm Oerlikon had quickly been identified as the deadliest antiaircraft weapon – one US Navy estimate stated it was responsible for 65 per cent of Japanese aircraft shot down in 1942. Accordingly, the US Navy increased the light antiaircraft batteries on early-war combatants. This was facilitated by unexpectedly high levels of production for the

OERLIKON 20mm CANNON

The US Navy's primary light antiaircraft weapon during the Pacific War was the 20mm Oerlikon gun, with a total of 88,000 — in both single and twin-mount versions — being produced during the conflict. The weapon was approved for US Navy production in November 1940 at the urging of the Royal Navy, which had adopted it in 1937. It took several months to get the gun into production, and it was still in short supply when the US Navy was forced into war in December 1941.

The choice of the 20mm Oerlikon was inspired. It had many positive attributes including a high rate of fire, a steady mount which increased accuracy, and it needed no external power so could be bolted down on both large ships and small wherever there was a clear arc of fire.

This view shows an Oerlikon in action against an incoming IJNAF raid. The weapon required a crew of four, as seen here. The detachable magazine was fed from the top. It held 60 rounds that could all be expended in just 7.5

seconds. The gun was placed on a free-swinging mount. On the right side of the mount was a hand-wheel to raise or lower the entire weapon. The gunner pointed and trained the gun through a set of handle-bars and shoulder rests. Practice was key, since the gunner had to be able to lead the target in elevation and transverse in order to hit it. Aside from an open sight, the gunner relied on a tracer every fifth round to aid in spotting. From mid-1942 the Mk 14 gunsight entered service, which dramatically increased accuracy.

The weapon was key to US Navy shipboard air defenses. By early 1942, three companies were producing 3,250 guns per month to meet demand. Through to the end of September 1944, the 20mm Oerlikon was estimated to be responsible for 32 per cent of all Japanese aircraft shot down. Very late in the war the advent of the kamikaze revealed the Oerlikon's primary shortcoming — a lack of hitting power. From this point, the 40mm Bofors was the US Navy's preferred antiaircraft weapon.

This photograph was taken on October 26, 1942 at the height of the dive-bombing attack on *Enterprise* during the Battle of the Santa Cruz Islands. It graphically shows the intensity of antiaircraft fire that US naval ships could throw up by this stage of the Pacific War. The carrier is on the left side of the image, a destroyer is visible in the center and *South Dakota*, on the right side of the image, is firing its starboard-side 5in./38 battery, as marked by the bright flash. At least two D3A1s can be seen above *Enterprise*. (NHHC)

20mm single mount as early as December 1941, and by the fact that the weapon needed no external power requirements and could be bolted onto ships wherever there was a clear arc of fire.

American efforts to augment the antiaircraft batteries of frontline ships and provide adequate training paid obvious dividends as evidenced by the mounting Japanese aircraft losses in 1942. In the second half of that year, the US Navy estimated that more than 48 per cent of IJNAF aircraft losses were attributable to 20mm fire, only 35 per cent to 5./38 fire, and just over one per cent to the 40mm gun, which was just entering service. While the 20mm gun shot down most Japanese aircraft in 1942, it was not long-ranged enough to destroy them before they had dropped their weapon in many cases. The US Navy was disappointed with the performance of its 5in./38 guns, which possessed the potential to down enemy aircraft before they could employ their weapons.

Under actual wartime conditions, however, the potential of the 5in./38 gun was often left unrealized because the target was not picked up in time to allow an engagement at extended ranges. In 1942 all 5in./38 rounds used the Mk 18 timed fuse. By the second half of 1943, 25 per cent used the VT fuse, which greatly increased the effectiveness of the 5in./38 gun. By the last six months of 1943, it was responsible for downing the most Japanese aircraft, and the 20mm weapon accounted for only 28 per cent of kills.

In summary, US Navy antiaircraft defenses were unable to protect the carriers in 1942. This was clearly shown by the fact that three were lost during the four carrier battles fought that year, all mainly because IJNAF torpedo-bombers were able to hit their targets. However, it is fair to state that the four carrier battles of 1942 provided the basis for the US Navy's successful air defenses in 1943–45 against conventional air attack.

AFTERMATH

The carrier battles of 1942 spelled the end of Japan's highly-trained pre-war cadre of carrier aircrewmen. Of the 765 who had participated in the Pearl Harbor attack, the 1942 carrier battles resulted in the estimated deaths of 409.

The Japanese were forced to evacuate Guadalcanal in January–February 1943, although that did not signal the end of the attrition for IJNAF carrier- and land-based units. American forces pressed against Japanese defenses in the Central and then the Northern Solomons to isolate the IJN's bastion of Rabaul. To stop the American advance, Adm Yamamoto sent his carrier air groups to Rabaul to combine with the land-based air force already there to form a strike force of some 350 aircraft. Despite its impressive size, the results of the Operation *I-Go* against Allied targets on Guadalcanal and New Guinea were meager and 50 aircraft were lost.

Yamamoto himself was killed on April 18, 1943, and his successor, Adm Mineichi Koga, again moved the carrier air groups from Truk to Rabaul in November of that

From 1943 the American advance in the Pacific was spearheaded by Essex-class carriers, 14 of them seeing action in-theater before the end of the war. The Essex-class was an extremely effective design, featuring a large air group, a heavy antiaircraft battery, and a high degree of survivability. None were sunk during the war, although several were badly damaged, including two that almost sank. This is USS *Essex* (CV-9) en route to raid Marcus Island on August 30, 1943. (NHHC)

A land-based B6N1 from the 531st Kokutai suffers a direct hit from a 5./38 shell fired from USS *Yorktown* (CV-10) during an unsuccessful torpedo attack on the carrier off Kwajalein on December 4, 1943. The 531st Kokutai was the first frontline unit to be issued with the new B6N1 torpedo-bomber, examples arriving during August 1943. Although the aircraft was better than the B5N2, it had little chance of penetrating the US Navy's Hellcat fighter CAP and layered antiaircraft fire. (NHHC)

same year to support the incumbent 11th Air Fleet. Their transfer was code-named Operation *Ro-Go*, and it allowed the IJNAF to mass 365 aircraft to attack US Navy shipping and other targets. The subsequent operations of these fighters and bombers are little known, but the lack of concrete results achieved by them clearly demonstrated the growing ineffectiveness of the IJNAF's attack units.

On November 1, 173 carrier aircraft arrived at Rabaul. The following day, 100 of them attacked a US Navy force of four light cruisers and eight destroyers. The ships had little in the way of friendly fighter support during the opening part of the battle, but they were all new and boasted multiple 5in./38, 40mm, and 20mm batteries paired with the latest fire control. The ships assumed an antiaircraft formation and began engaging the approaching Japanese at 14,000 yards with 5in./38 guns. The task force was well-handled, unlike the dive-bombers, which attacked in an erratic fashion. Gunners claimed 17 shot down, and in return the IJNAF was only able to place two hits on the stern of the USS *Montpelier* (CL-57), which caused little damage.

The US Navy's emphasis on antiaircraft exercises and the obviously diminished skills of the Japanese aviators had rendered the unexpected outcome of a task force with virtually no fighter cover fighting off a major air attack with almost no damage.

On November 11 the IJNAF was able to launch a full strike against an American carrier force attacking Rabaul. The latter, Task Group 50.3, consisted of the fleet carriers USS *Essex* (CV-9) and USS *Bunker Hill* (CV-17), the light carrier USS *Independence* (CVL-22) and a weak screen of only nine destroyers. After the carrier aircraft struck naval targets in Rabaul in the morning, they braced for the expected counterattack. The Japanese assault was comprised of 67 fighters escorting 27 D3A2 and 14 B5N2s, followed by some G4Ms. American fighter interception was ineffective until the dive-bombers began their attacks, so it came down to the antiaircraft fire from the three carriers grouped together in a 2,000-yard circle, with the destroyers in a second circle at 4,000 yards from the formation center. *Bunker Hill* was the main Japanese target. All three carriers were near missed by the 20 dive-bombers that attacked, only three of which escaped. The B5N2s followed, and all 14 were shot down without recording any success.

This virtually unknown battle had several important ramifications. It was the first major IJNAF air attack on a US Navy carrier group since Santa Cruz and the first on the new Essex-class carriers. The results showed that the balance of power between Japanese maritime attack air units and US Navy carrier groups had decisively altered in favor of the Americans. Furthermore, the losses suffered by the Japanese carrier air groups sent down to Rabaul on November 1 were crippling – 50 per cent of fighters, 85 per cent of dive-bombers, and 50 per cent of torpedo-bombers. This meant that the IJN's carrier force was not ready when US forces invaded the Gilbert Islands later in November. Not until mid-June 1944 when the Americans invaded the Mariana Islands did the IJN commit its carrier force again.

The IJN frantically rebuilt its carrier force in expectation of the next major American offensive. By June 1944, the Japanese had assembled nine carriers and equipped them with more than 400 aircraft, including the replacements for the B5N (the Nakajima B6N "Jill" torpedo-bomber) and the D3A (the Yokosuka D4Y1 "Judy"). This seemingly powerful force was much less capable than it appeared since a number of its aviators had barely received six months of training. Some, in fact, had only completed two or three months of flying on frontline types.

By June 1944, the US Navy had widened the gap between its fleet air defense capabilities and the capabilities of IJNAF attack aircraft. The new F6F Hellcat fighter could lay waste to incoming Japanese strikes when properly directed by radar. The numbers of carriers had also increased, and in June 1944 the Pacific Fleet fielded seven fleet and eight light carriers for the invasion of the Marianas. These were organized into four task forces and given a heavy escort of battleships, cruisers, and destroyers.

The massed antiaircraft fire of these task forces was highly effective. Each Essex-class carrier carried up to 12 5in./38 guns and 18 quad 40mm mounts, together with as many as 58 single 20mm guns. Battleships were also impressive antiaircraft platforms with 20 5in./38 guns, at least 15 quad 40mm mounts, and 48 or more 20mm guns. Newly constructed heavy and light cruisers were fitted with 12 5in./38 guns, 11 quad 40mm mounts, and more than 20 20mm guns. Even a Fletcher-class destroyer of the period had five 5in./38 guns and six twin 40mm guns.

The US Navy also fielded the best radars and fire control systems available. Information from all sensors was fed into a central location called the combat information center, which collated all available data and decided the best course of action to protect the ship or task force.

Another American technological innovation which had tremendous implications for fleet air defense was the deployment of the VT fuse in January 1943. It emitted radio waves that were reflected off the target to provide the shell with the precise moment when to explode in order to cause the most damage to the enemy aircraft.

Among the IJNAF aircraft that broke through the US Navy CAP on June 19, 1944 were several B6Ns from the second Japanese raid. These attempted to attack *Enterprise*, but failed to score a hit. Note the small splash in the center of this view, which marks where one of the aircraft crashed into the water. The light carrier at right is either USS *Princeton* (CVL-23) or USS *San Jacinto* (CVL-30). (NHHC)

The Essex-class carrier USS *Bunker Hill* (CV-17) came under attack on June 19, 1944 from several D4Y dive-bombers from the second IJNAF raid of the Battle of the Philippine Sea. The only damage inflicted by the Japanese aircraft was from this near miss, which caused minor damage and killed three crewmen. The aircraft that had just dropped its bomb is visible to the left, minus its tail, and it is headed into the water. (NHHC)

This made the process of plotting antiaircraft fire much easier, since all that was required was to get the shell near the target and let the fuse do the rest.

The US Navy's new air defense system translated into a high degree of invulnerability against conventional Japanese air attack.

When the rebuilt IJN carrier force met its US Navy counterpart on June 19, the results were predictable. The IJNAF aircraft possessed greater range than their American counterparts, and combined with the cautious nature of the TF 58 commander, Adm Raymond A. Spruance, gave the Japanese the first strike. They used this opportunity to launch four waves from their nine carriers that involved no fewer than 326 aircraft. Had this been 1942, such a massive first strike would have assured a Japanese victory. But by 1944, the paradigm of the first strike guaranteeing victory had disappeared.

The primary agent of the destruction of Japanese air power on June 19 was the Hellcat, not antiaircraft fire. Nevertheless, the Grumman fighters could not provide total protection from such a large attack, so as many as 50 IJNAF "Judy" dive-bombers and "Jill" torpedo-bombers broke through to attack the carrier force. The results were beyond disappointing for the Japanese. Only a single bomb hit an American ship, and this was literally in the worst place possible, since it struck the heavily-armored turret of a battleship and caused little damage. Two carriers were near missed but damage was light.

Japanese pilots failed to keep formation and deliver coordinated attacks and their aim was abysmal. Of the 326 aircraft launched on the four strikes, only 97 returned to their carriers. By the end of the following day, when the US Navy executed its own attack on the IJN carriers, only 35 of the original complement of just over 400 IJNAF aircraft remained.

The Battle of the Philippine Sea marked the IJN's last attempt to mount major conventional air attacks on US Navy ships. For the rest of the war the emphasis shifted to "special attack" (*kamikaze*) operations, providing the final testimony on the effectiveness of US Navy fleet air defenses.

FURTHER READING

Campbell, John, *Naval Weapons of World War Two* (Naval Institute Press, Annapolis, Maryland, 2002)

Chambers, Mark with Holmes, Tony, *Osprey Combat Aircraft 119 – Nakajima B5N 'Kate' and B6N 'Jill' Units* (Osprey Publishing, Oxford, 2017)

Claringbould, Michael and Ingman, Peter, *South Pacific Air War Volume 1* (Avonmore Books, Kent Town, South Australia, 2017)

Claringbould, Michael and Ingman, Peter, *South Pacific Air War Volume 3* (Avonmore Books, Kent Town, South Australia, 2019)

Francillon, René J., *Japanese Aircraft of the Pacific War* (Naval Institute Press, Annapolis, Maryland, 1987)

Friedman, Norman, *Naval Antiaircraft Guns and Gunnery* (Naval Institute Press, Annapolis, Maryland, 2013)

Harms, Norman E., *Hard Lesson Vol. 1 US Naval Campaigns Pacific Theater February 1942–1943* (Scale Specialties, Garden Grove, California, 1987)

Lundstrom, John B., *The First Team* (Naval Institute Press, Annapolis, Maryland, 1984)

Lundstrom, John B., *The First Team and the Guadalcanal Campaign* (Naval Institute Press, Annapolis, Maryland, 1994)

Morison, Samuel Eliot, *Breaking the Bismarck Barrier 22 July 1942–1 May 1944* (Little, Brown and Company, Boston, Massachusetts, 1975)

Peattie, Mark R., *Sunburst* (Naval Institute Press, Annapolis, Maryland, 2001)

Reynolds, Clark G., *The Fast Carriers* (Naval Institute Press, Annapolis, Maryland, 1992)

Smith, Peter C., *Fist from the Sky* (Stackpole Books, Mechanicsburg, Pennsylvania, 2006)

Stafford, Edward P., *The Big E* (Naval Institute Press, Annapolis, 2015)

Stille, Mark, *Osprey Campaign 214 – The Coral Sea 1942* (Osprey Publishing, Oxford, 2009)

Stille, Mark, *Osprey Campaign 226 – Midway 1942* (Osprey Publishing, Oxford, 2010)

Stille, Mark, *Osprey Campaign 247 – Santa Cruz 1942* (Osprey Publishing, Oxford, 2012)

Stille, Mark, *Osprey Campaign 313 – The Philippine Sea 1944* (Osprey Publishing, Oxford, 2017)

Tagaya, Osamu, *Osprey Combat Aircraft 22 – Mitsubishi Type 1 Rikko "Betty" Units of World War 2* (Osprey Publishing, Oxford, 2001)

Tagaya, Osamu, *Osprey Combat Aircraft 63 – Aichi 99 Kanbaku "Val" Units 1937–42* (Osprey Publishing, Oxford, 2011)

INDEX

Page numbers in **bold** refer to illustrations and their captions.